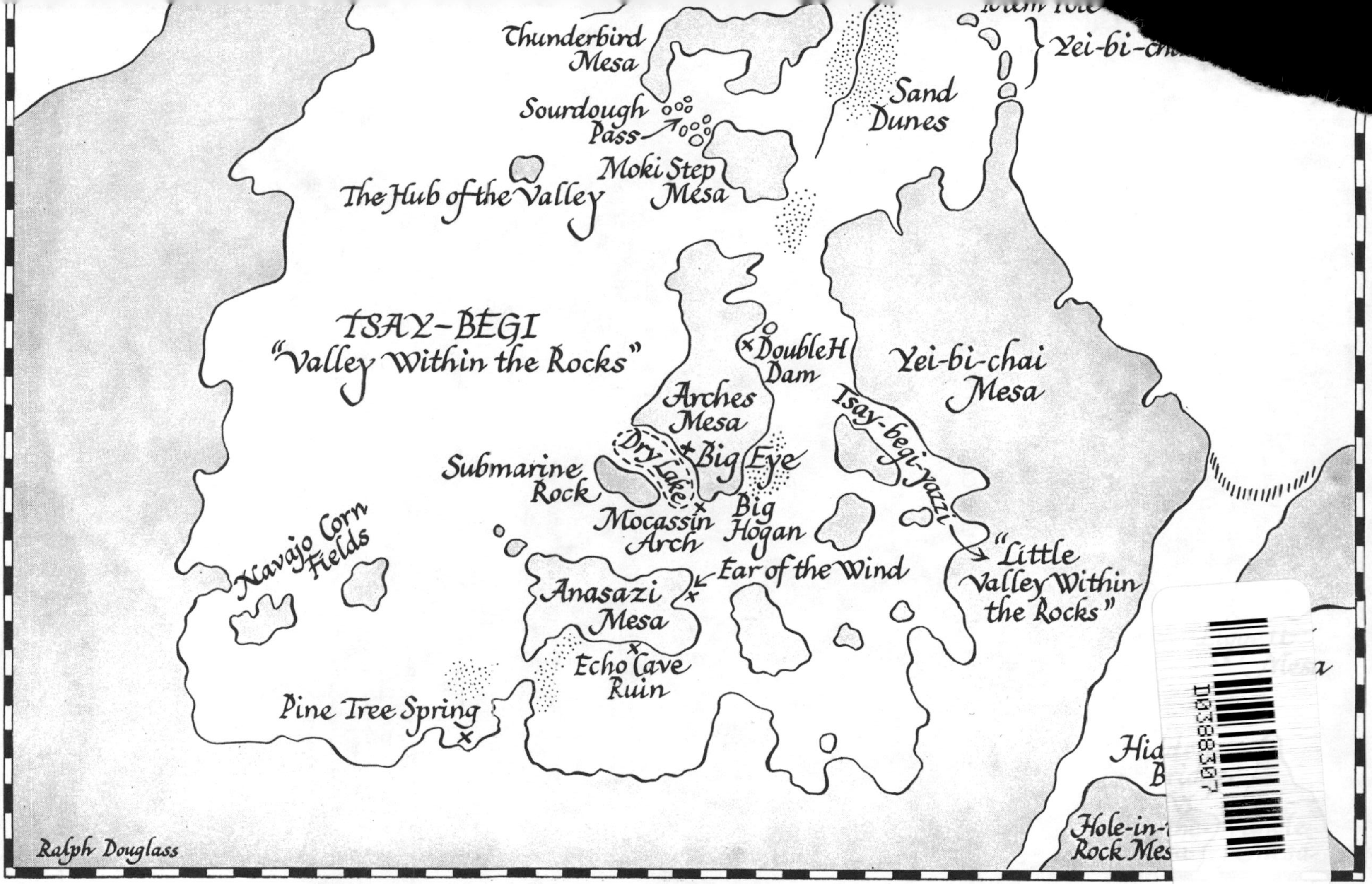

Thunderbird
Mesa

Sourdough
Pass

Moki Step
Mesa

The Hub of the Valley

Sand
Dunes

Yei-bi-chai
Mesa

Tsay-begi-yazzi

"Little
Valley Within
the Rocks"

DoubleH
Dam

Arches
Mesa

Big Eye

Big
Hogan

Ear of the Wind

Dry Lake

Mocassin
Arch

TSAY–BEGI
"Valley Within the Rocks"

Submarine
Rock

Anasazi
Mesa

Echo Cave
Ruin

Pine Tree Spring

Navajo Corn
Fields

Yei-bi-chai

Hid
B

Hole-in-
Rock Mes

D0388307

Ralph Douglass

To Lois

The other dream come true...

LAND OF

ROOM ENOUGH
AND
TIME ENOUGH

Richard E. Klinck

PARISH
PUBLISHING
Heber City, Utah

1995

Previously published by Peregrine Smith Books
ISBN 0-87905-159-0

Parish Publishing
3150 W. 3600 So.
Heber City, UT 84032
ISBN 0-9646320-0-4

Cover photo and design by Michelle Parish

Printed in the U.S.A.

Library of Congress Information is on file with the publisher

FORWARD

LEGEND...

I was wandering. Mentally. And the phone rang. Monument Valley calling.

Appropriate. It seems to do that a lot. Irresistible. Calling since long before LAND OF ROOM ENOUGH AND TIME ENOUGH came out in 1953. Early on the Valley called me via the movies, but I didn't know where to find it. Then in 1949 I got help from a Chevron highway map, when they used to have little pictures across the bottom with corresponding numbers on the map. There it was, Monument Valley, and the number showed me where to go find it. So I did.

Since then I haven't needed either the picture or the map. It still calls, and I've always listened, and been back many times. Visiting that part of me which always lives there.

But this was a different call. Gerald LaFont from Goulding's Monument Valley Lodge. We'd like to reprint your book. It's historic. And we'd like to have you add a few pages to the new edition-give it an update.

Historic? But wasn't it only yesterday when I found that Chevron map? I checked back through the journals I've kept of each visit. Yes, Historic! Then the parade of images began.

It's been forty-five years since that young fellow from Iowa got the idea of using his fascination with Monument Valley to create a book that tried to tell its whole story. A collection of rejection slips, then the University of New Mexico Press said, "Yes, we'd like to publish...".

Actually, forty-five years shouldn't even be worth noting when laid down next to the timeless monuments. Just a mere whisper in time. The geologic chart doesn't accept increments that small. Nothing really changes in such an eternal place in a little less than half a century.

Or does it? In that tiny piece of time there have been a lot of additions to the human story. And with our limited vision that's what we notice most. From such a viewpoint Monument Valley has changed profoundly.

Pavement came – all the way, connecting Blanding on the north with Tuba City on the south. No more warning signs ("no gas available, carry water..."). No more sand traps and no more dusty journeys covering a few miles in lots of hours. The pavement meant you didn't have to really think about the journey anymore. You could just go. And lots did. No scarcity of visitors, far more than the few who came on a vision quest, or to realize a dream.

Then the railroad came north toward Kayenta in 1971 and the Peabody Coal began a series of major decisions on how things looked and were done. Kayenta got a bridge over the wash to the north, plus a Holiday Inn and a lot of other things. Now the mail was delivered to Goulding's – they didn't have to make a weekly trip in - and groceries were certainly no problem.

Monument Valley had been the star of nine of his finest movies when John Ford died in 1973. When John Wayne died in 1979 the Valley lost its starring role. Oh, it's appeared in a near-endless number of movies, television stories, and commercials – from being part of Chevy Chase's vacation, and back to the future with Michael J. Fox, to the place where Forrest Gump stopped running. But it's been a long time since Monument Valley was more than just a gimmick - a readily identifiable backdrop.

With the pavement came a flood of visitors and Harry and "Mike" Goulding made gradual changes in the Trading Post and Lodge. New buildings went up, gradually most of the old ones came down. There were new assistants and partners, and the Gouldings spent more time away from the Valley in Sun City and a few other locations.

Harry died April 4, 1981. A lot of us lost something very special that day. Mike eventually came back to the Valley as her home for awhile and she died on Thanksgiving Day, November 26, 1992.

It's hard to think of Monument Valley without Harry and Mike. In fact, I can't. One and the same.

The hospital improved, became a fine service as more and more Navajos moved into the area. A Good Sam Campground was added, and recently enlarged. The National Park vision was never realized, but a Navajo Tribal Park became a reality with a disconcerting pay booth controlling the now-paved entrance road. There's a campground there, too, on the Rim where Harry used to pause at sunset so we could get a last fill-up on Monument Valley magic.

In the early sixties Knox College took over the operation of the Lodge, with a Navajo Scholarship concept built in. After nineteen years the college sold the property and the LaFont brothers now continue the traditions.

At the junction where the Goulding's road leaves the main highway there's green grass and a modern high school. Nearby the super market is open everyday from 9 to 9 and you can rent videos, right about where John Wayne led the troops under thunder and lightning in SHE WORE A YELLOW RIBBON.

All these things are a part of our combined effort to make Monument Valley better. But despite the modern day facade, the wonderful valley still persists. And the following words might help explain the legend.

Richard E. Klinck
April 1995

The place where Forrest Gump stopped running
PHOTO BY MICHELLE PARISH

Lois, looking over Castle Butte group from near Monument Pass

PHOTOGRAPH BY RICHARD E. KLINCK

Muley Point at sunrise, Monument Valley in far distance
PHOTOGRAPH BY RICHARD E. KLINCK

THE SEARCHERS - John Wayne coming out of Chief Scar's tent, Ford far left
PHOTOGRAPH BY RICHARD E. KLINCK

Looking northeast from the center of the Valley
PHOTOGRAPH BY RICHARD E. KLINCK

Sunset, Monument Valley

PHOTOGRAPHER UNKNOWN

Purple Shadows

PHOTOGRAPH BY W.L. RUSHO

Navajo woman in Monument Valley

The Mittens

PHOTOGRAPH BY W.L. RUSHO

PREFACE

I am gratified to know that *Land of Room Enough and Time Enough* is once again in print. I have long felt that this is the most informative and interesting book on Monument Valley yet written. Richard Klinck would be pleased to know that his personal expression of love of the Valley and the Navajos is once again available.

Richard's first visit to Monument Valley's Goulding's Trading Post, which my husband and I had homesteaded, was at the very end of his vacation. As he stood by the front door and gazed out over the magnificent scenery in our "front yard" he was awestruck. He knew he had to return soon. He told me then that he was going to write a book about what he had seen.

True to his promise, he did return, time and time again. And he did write his book. The word about the wonders of Monument Valley has spread and thousands of visitors now come to discover for themselves the ageless monoliths of stone and the rich cultural heritage of the land's inhabitants. I love the land and its people and cherish my memories of the Land of Room Enough and Time Enough.

"Mike" Goulding

CONTENTS

A VALLEY IS BORN

In the beginning, it was all darkness. And there was nothing. Then from the nothing came a burst of light, and into the light came our world, strange and misshapen. It burned and pulsated, hanging molten, waiting for great hands to press it into form and substance. And so Time — endless, eternal Time — laid out the plans for creation, then followed them explicitly.

Monument Valley is young as geologic time goes. But not as we know and understand time. We are a people born of time. To us it is great and all-important. We wake at a certain hour and our first thought is about time. Did we wake early or late? We catch a bus or streetcar, one that runs more or less on a schedule with time. We work, we play, we sleep, always governed by time. Ever so slowly, time ticks away our lives and we watch them flow away with regret.

When we go back into time, our perception fades. A few years we can remember well. For a few decades we can recall memories that tell much of what has happened to us in *our* years. But to reach before that we must open a book, to read there of what came a hundred, two hundred, a thousand years earlier.

Then time loses shape and is overcome by change. It is still time, because we continue to measure it in numbers of years. But grouped together in great numbers we cannot comprehend, we lose sight of its relative meaning. We no longer can recognize it as something we know. It loses identity with us and our present.

But try to ride back into time. Forget its hours and days and years. Think in terms of eons and watch what has happened in the past. Lose yourself in the maze of time that envelops every one of us. What does a million years mean? How can our frail minds grasp anything so vast and so complex as a million years? What can we compare to a million years to get an idea of its boundlessness? There is nothing. A million years is beyond our perception. We are so small, so unimportant, so powerless in the face of time. We cannot even realize the immensity of a million years, and yet, as we delve back into time we find that our earth is perhaps two billion years old! We say it— two billion—but it has no meaning. Two billion we cannot understand. Still, that was the beginning when all was fluid and aflame.

Half of that time fled. A billion years passed and still there was no trace of life upon our world, nor did the earth in any way resemble the land we know. It was a billion years of planned creation by wind and rain, white heat and explosive internal forces, plus Him of the Master Design. Successive stages of the earth's history held sway, faded, and were lost forever.

But stay by your vigil in time. Years—millions of years—flared by, some in flames, some bound in ice. Then, less than 25,000,000 years ago, Monument Valley was about to be spawned. With only a brief glance at the eternal plans, Creation took a slight 25,000,000 years and used it to carve this wonderland. Even that, without being compared to the wholeness of geologic time, is too great, too vast, for us to understand. In a thousand years there is very little visible change in the valley of the monuments. What does it mean beside your life and mine? Set your mind to work in millions of years, if you can, and then you'll see why Monument Valley must be called eternal.

The scientists and geologists of our time have delved deeply into the earth's secrets and have given strange names to the five chapters they find buried there. Archaeozoic, Proterozoic, Paleozoic, Mesozoic, and Cenozoic— strange and unfamiliar names, but each embracing great periods of time, and each highly important in the history of our earth. Not until very late in geologic history—not until the Pleistocene epoch of the Cenozoic era, even as man was being readied for his entrance upon earth, was Monument Valley being fashioned.

Before that, during the Paleozoic and Mesozoic eras, parts of the North

American continent were periodically submerged beneath the waters of ancient seas. Portions of the land we know as our United States were covered with water from time to time. There were none of the landmarks we have come to be familiar with today. It was another world, a far away and primeval world, but parent of today.

During the Permian period, which came at the close of the Paleozoic era, a particularly vast inundation of land occurred. It included the land to the immediate west of Monument Valley and the period was marked by the deposition of a layer of limestone now termed the Kaibab limestone. It was laid down in great quantities of red-bed sediments that had eroded from the Colorado mountains to the east. This layer of so-called Kaibab limestone did not extend into Monument Valley itself. Today, it has been found to thin and disappear completely just to the west of the valley. This means that Permian waters never touched Monument Valley, though they did come very close. Instead, the red beds, that is, the erodings from the Colorado peaks, remained on the surface in the region of the valley of the monuments and later were to be identified with the name of De Chelly sandstone, a name that corresponds almost identically with the Coconino sandstone which geologists have found under the Kaibab limestone in the Grand Canyon area.

Another era passed. It was not until the close of the Cretaceous period, at the end of the Mesozoic era that the waters began to advance again. This later-day intrusion culminated in one of the greatest floods of all time. Almost fifty per cent of the North American continent was submerged, including the areas of northern Arizona and southern Utah. After relaxing their hold for many millions of years, the seas came back, again covering and overwhelming the land. But at length, as in the past, these seas, vast though they were, either retreated or were silted up. And from the close of the Mesozoic era, seventy million years ago, until today, the area that includes Monument Valley was above water. It was still to be the subject of the many geologic phenomena of upheaval, faulting, and tearing, but the seas never again touched it.

It was the years that followed hard on the heels of the Mesozoic era, a time identified as the Cenozoic era, that witnessed the complete shaping of the present Monument Valley. The hard outer crust of the earth's surface was battered, broken, and punctured by the restless forces that were swirling about on the inside. The intensity of heat, reacting upon water and rock,

— GEOLOGIC TIME TABLE —

Era	Period / Epoch	Rocks of these periods completely eroded away during Pleistocene carving	Rocks exposed in M. V.	Rocks still buried in Monument Valley. To be exposed later?
CENOZOIC (MODERN TIMES)	PLEISTOCENE	Wind and water begin carving Monument Valley. Man makes entrance on earth		
	PLIOCENE			
	MIOCENE	Second (present) generation of Rocky Mountains born		
	OLIGOCENE			
	EOCENE	Ancient Rocky Mountains worn down. Sediments carried west and deposited in Monument Valley area. Sea has retreated		
	PALEOCENE			
MESOZOIC	UPPER CRETACEOUS			
	LOWER CRETACEOUS	Monument Valley completely submerged. Rocky Mountains thrust up to east and begin to erode away		
	JURASSIC			
	TRIASSIC			
PALEOZOIC	PERMIAN		Inundation of area west of Monument Valley. Kaibab limestone deposited on top of Coconino (De Chelly) sandstone in area covered by water	
	PENNSYLVANIAN			
	MISSISSIPPIAN			
	DEVONIAN			Continent subjected to repeated submergings, faultings, and upheavals. Topographic features not yet established as we know them
	SILURIAN			
	ORDOVICIAN			
	CAMBRIAN			
	PROTEROZOIC			
	ARCHAEOZOIC			

caused vast changes across the land. It was a period typified by terrible earthquakes that created new ranges of mountains. The Mesozoic era was finally ushered to a violent ending that resulted in the thrusting up of the Rocky Mountains. The Colorado Plateau, a table-like area which features the valley of the monuments a bit south of its center, was not deformed by this cataclysmic action to the east, but it was profoundly affected by the aftereffects.

The first generation of Rocky Mountains in Colorado were gradually worn down by the relentless forces of erosion. During the Eocene epoch of the Cenozoic era, huge quantities of these Rocky Mountain sediments were deposited in the section of land that now contains Monument Valley. They topped the Permian red beds, concealing all traces of that red sandstone. Then, during the Miocene epoch, which followed the Eocene years, a new upheaval came, and the present Rocky Mountains were born.

About that same time, a regional uplift occurred on the Colorado Plateau. The entire table-top area, covering a number of thousands of square miles,

Rising 1,225 feet above the surrounding plain, Agathlan is, perhaps, the most conspicuous landmark in the Valley.

PHOTOGRAPHER UNKNOWN

was pushed upward by the pressure from below. It buckled upward for several thousand feet, until the plateau surface was rather profoundly faulted, that is, broken and cracked, so that it no longer retained its comparative smoothness. This faulting started a whole new cycle of erosion, which, in turn, widened and deepened the newly created rifts, eventually making them into canyons. The irresistible forces of wind and water took over and began their tremendous job of shaping the valley of the monuments.

Rivers and streams, starting from tiny rivulets of water offered by ancient rainstorms, buried themselves in the Eocene sediments and, aided by the winds, completely erased all traces of the later geologic periods. All the deposits of the Cenozoic era were washed and worn away. The tons of sediment which had carefully been moved in from that first generation of Rockies were moved again and deposited elsewhere. Then the rocks of the Mesozoic era felt the relentless wear of the elements and vanished without trace. The wind and the rain ate far back into the very beginning of Mesozoic time, baring the red rocks of the pristine Triassic years. A thousand or more feet of silt and rock were borne away, probably to the San Juan and Colorado rivers, to be carried by them to the southern seas. Then another thousand feet of the living rock was completely washed away, leaving only the hard, resistent portions to form the fabulous red rock monuments that reside there today. And it required the bulk of 25,000,000 years to achieve this majestic example of nature's architecture.

There was also volcanic action in the eternal valley during the infinite period of carving. Alhambra Rock and Agathlan* Peak, as well as lesser points in the same general area, give visible proof that tremendous forces were unleashed up on the surface there in the valley of the monuments. But even cinder cones and vast lava flows that perhaps once covered thousands of square miles of the Colorado Plateau country have been washed away by the more relentless, though not as suddenly violent, forces of wind and rain, those forces that have no regard for time. All that is left are the black, igneous volcanic conduits, the very sources of the lava flow itself, stripped to the world and rising now like forgotten towers of midnight, the sole remains of the molten fluids that once filled the craters, then hardened when the internal forces rested and slept. Now they are only tombstones, monuments to past furies that swept through the valley of the monuments.

The monuments themselves are carved from rocks of the Cutler forma-

---

* This is the spelling in general use, although most government maps spell it "Agathla."—Ed.

Eroded gulch

tion, a group of deposits made during the Permian period, and they are capped with rocks that were laid down during the Triassic age. Once these rocks were buried far below the surface, then were brought to sunshine once more when the rocks above them were eroded away.

TABLE OF FORMATIONS

	Jurassic		
Triassic	Upper Triassic	Chinle Formation Shinarump Conglomerate	
	Lower Triassic	Moenkopi Formation	
Permian		Cutler Formation	Hoskinnini Tongue De Chelly Sandstone Member Organ Rock Tongue Cedar Mesa Sandstone Member Halgaito Tongue
		Rico Formation	
Pennsylvanian			

This Cutler formation is divided into five distinct subdivisions, all having particular significance and meaning to the geologist. Three subdivisions, from the oldest to the youngest, are the Halgaito tongue, Cedar Mesa sandstone member, Organ Rock tongue, De Chelly sandstone member, and the Hoskinnini tongue. The latter two, or perhaps three, correspond in age to the Kaibab limestone, thus indicating that they were carried into Monument Valley and surrounding country and deposited there about the same time the area to the west was covered by a great Permian sea. The Cedar Mesa and De Chelly sandstones probably converge into one unit to the west, and then become identical with the Coconino sandstone of the Grand Canyon. It is this De Chelly sandstone member of the Cutler formation that crops out in the monuments of the enchanted valley. It is not particularly resistant to erosion and rarely forms isolated spires unless protected by a more durable capping of the younger, more weather-resistant, beds. If it is not protected by these later deposits it usually is weathered into rounded forms, closely resembling the sand dunes they may once have been. The Hoskinnini tongue is practically coincident with the De Chelly sandstone. It crops out in some of the monuments, but is so close to the De Chelly member in appearance and texture that, usually, it is unrecognizable.

The Moenkopi formation, with rocks that date back to Lower Triassic times, is the oldest and lowest of the Mesozoic formations and crops out near the tops of the monuments immediately beneath the thin, resistant cap known as Shinarump conglomerate. The Moenkopi deposits are of a deeper color than the underlying De Chelly sandstone, and provide the flaming colors that are so characteristically beautiful in Monument Valley at sunset. It is easily reduced by erosion when not capped, as are the De Chelly deposits, but usually shows in a steep slope when found beneath the durable Shinarump topping. Often the cliffs formed in these instances are unscalable, creating buttes whose flat tops cannot be explored.

Silicified, or petrified, logs are quite plentiful in the Shinarump deposits and are found frequently in the Monument Valley area. In Piute mythology, the silicified logs were held to be the weapons of Shinarav, the Great Wolf God. Accumulated masses, such as those in the Petrified Forest National Monument, near Winslow, Arizona, are regarded as battlefields where the Piute god challenged his foes. This Piute tale corresponds remarkably well with a similar Navajo legend. Major Powell suggested the name of Shinarump, meaning "weapons of Shinarav," as being most appropriate for the deposits containing the silicified materials. The name was immediately adopted and has been used since.

Camel Butte

PHOTOGRAPH BY RONALD W. HARRIS

Today it is hard to comprehend the gigantic forces that have been at work in the valley. With its arid climate, Monument Valley seems to be anything but a region that was once a vast inland sea where water lapped at swampy shores, and rivers and streams once washed away hundreds of square miles of red sandstone. But in actuality and practice, the mighty forces are there still.

You can watch Nature unleash one of its powerful tools when a great thunderstorm invades the valley. Dormant washes suddenly become alive as silt-filled waters pour down them. Waterfalls spring from everywhere. And the companion tool, never-dying wind, is there still, too, continuing to take its slow but eternal toll on the monuments. But even though you watch carefully you cannot see the effects. The valley of the monuments looks today almost as it did at the time of Christ. There have been only minor changes. After all, what is two thousand years compared to twenty-five million?

After the cloudless skies have returned to the valley, when the rain gods have fled, and the wind breathes only softly, man makes his mighty efforts to restore the scene to his liking. His roads are graded and the obstructing washes are filled. But Nature smiles and watches without concern. There's another twenty-five million years just around the corner. She has plenty of time. . . .

THE FIRST PEOPLE

As Time and Creation yawned and settled back on their haunches, thinking of something new to design, Man entered upon the scene. Tiny, insignificant Man, coming so very late in the story of the world's history. It was many centuries before the dawn of the Christian era that roving bands of hunters from the Old World crossed the ice-bound waters of Bering Strait, to wander freely through a new and uninhabited continent. Who they were, what they were like, and exactly where they came from we will, perhaps, never know. But we do know that some of these wanderers probably roved into the Southwest; for localities in Nevada, New Mexico, and Colorado have been discovered where various artifacts lie together with the bones of prehistoric bison, sloths, and other animals. What must they have thought if they wandered into the vast and virgin silence of Monument Valley? Certainly it was even more strange and unreal to them than it is to us of today.

The traces and clues left by prehistoric animals can be more easily and clearly pieced together to tell their story that can be the remains left behind by the early man of a corresponding period. Bones of the Western ground sloth, ancient relative of the South American tree sloth of today, and a member of the group of mammals that includes the anteater and the armadillo, have been located in limestone caverns not far from Monument Valley. This ancient animal roamed throughout the canyon country of southern

11

Utah and northern Arizona, and the Southwest. He wandered about as a member of a small herd, feeding on plants. Long, in-curved claws indicate that he walked on only the outside toes of the front feet and put most of his weight on the huge hind feet. He inhabited the region about 10,000 years ago.

Other animals which have been found in various deposits, preserved by a fortunate combination of climate and chance, include the mammoth, an extinct type of elephant, teeth and tusks of which were found in the deposits of Charley Day Spring, near Tuba City. Camels and diminutive horses also lived in the area.

But before we can locate definite proof of a people in the valley and look upon the relics of their civilization, we must move up in time to the period when Christ taught in Palestine. As Christianity was building its noble foundation, primitive inhabitants of northern Arizona and southern Utah, as well as adjacent portions of Colorado, New Mexico, Nevada, and Utah began to raise corn. These people formed the first link in a long history of a culture that still survives in a modified form.

The Navajos call these people the Anasazi, which means the Ancients or the First People. And the initial phase of the Anasazi is known as the Basket Maker period. The peoples of the Basket Maker society were fairly common in the Monument Valley area. But remember that common is another of those words that must be looked upon with care. There were many people for that particular era. Perhaps two hundred of them lived in the valley of the monuments and adjacent territories. After their gradual evolution from caves, the people lived in pit houses, which were partly above ground and partly below. By a haphazard arrangement of poles, twigs, and mud an igloo effect was achieved. These were the first residences of Monument Valley. Look at the hogan of the present-day Navajo and you will see what little change has actually taken place in Monument Valley architecture in almost two thousand years.

The Basket Makers developed the art of basket weaving to a high degree, but they had no pottery until late in their period, when the ceramic arts were greatly improved with the invention of fired pottery. On these crude bowls were painted black designs on a grey background. They did not possess the bow and arrow, though they did have the atlatl, a notched stick used in throwing darts. They made square-toed sandals from yucca and other fibers, created twine-woven bags and rabbit-fur robes. Fine workmanship was exhibited in stone, shell, and bone, and they developed an agriculture in maize, squash, and beans, though they still depended to a great extent upon wild vegetable foods and products of the chase. The turkey was domesticated, as well as the dog.

The end of the Basket Maker periods came when a new physical type migrated into the land. With them came the custom of artificially flattening the back of the head by strapping every baby to his cradleboard during the first years of his life. These people filtered in in ever-increasing numbers and became assimilated into the old society as long as it existed.

The new society is called Pueblo I or Developmental Pueblo. Pottery technique improved again. Plain and black-on-white vessels continued to be made, but, in addition to these, there came jars produced in a manner that gave a banded appearance to the neck of the finished item.

The Pueblo peoples covered a much more extensive area than did their forerunners. From the Colorado River to Texas are found remnants of the Pueblo period. In the south and west, the pit-type dwelling continued, but the pits were dug deeper. Entrance was gained by a ladder which entered the subterranean room through the smoke hole. Homes of these people are found at various points throughout the Monument Valley area. The Juniper Cove ruin, eight miles west of Kayenta, on the border of the Monument Valley country, provides a notable example of the pit house.

From A.D. 900 to about A.D. 1000 these people lived among the monuments. Cotton was added to the list of cultivated plants and was woven into garments. Cooking utensils of black pottery seem to have been quite common. They were made of coils of clay built upon one another in succession. In most cases, the product was smoothed off afterwards so that all evidence of coiling was destroyed. But in some of the pottery of this particular period the sides were not smoothed, leaving a rough spiral finish. This type, identified as corrugated ware, continued in use until about A.D. 1400.

As the civilization progressed, so did the art of home building. Houses of stone and adobe and clay were built above the ground. They were one story high and contained from six to fourteen rooms. Shaped like an L or U, these houses were known as clan houses. The pit-house structure was not discarded but remained as the kiva—the underground ceremonial chamber, or "church." It has been remarked by some authorities that the kiva is one of the most striking archaeological features of the Southwest. No village was ever without at least one and usually there were several. Round or square, access was always gained through the smoke hole.

The Great Pueblo period, with a vague beginning somewhere between A.D. 1000 and 1100, was characterized by a tendency of the people to gather in large terraced pueblos of three or four stories. These dwellings often were located in great shallow caves in the faces of the sheer red rock cliffs. Betatakin and Keet Seel cliff dwellings of the Navajo National Monument are notable examples of this period. What caused the people to move into their new homes is a subject for serious conjecture. Many say that it was because of the influx of a new people, an invader, probably the Navajo. But the very fact that the Navajo legends contain no mention of these earlier people, and that they often regard the cliff dwellings as the homes of their own gods, seem basically to contradict the invader theory.

The Great Pueblo period waned toward the end of the thirteenth century and eventually all the villages were abandoned. Here again is a puzzling

Anasazi ruin in Monument Valley

PHOTOGRAPHER UNKNOWN

question. What caused this great exodus? Most historians seem to agree that, in this case, it was because of a long period of drought that parched the country for twenty-three successive years, from 1276 to 1299. Or, as before, maybe it was because of the approach of the engulfing tide of Navajos and Apaches. Whatever the cause, the people moved southward, where they resumed their civilization, but without the ancient culture and comparative degree of perfection they had once known.

The empire continued in other parts of the Southwest and passed through two subsequent periods. Pueblo Four, or Regressive Pueblo, was the first of these. It lasted from approximately A.D. 1300 to A.D. 1700, and was followed by the Historical Pueblo period, extending from A.D. 1700 to the present. The modern descendants of the ancients can be seen today in the Hopi villages of Arizona, and Zuñi, Ácoma, and the Rio Grande pueblos of New Mexico.

And so an ancient civilization lived and died in Monument Valley. Its glory was limited, but its people must have been majestically happy. Imagine, if you can, a lifetime of the magnificent sunrises and sunsets that are to be found only among the monuments. Imagine the beauty of moonlight and the soft touch of a cool desert breeze in the darkness. Yes, the Anasazi must have been simply, but perfectly, happy.

Scientists have long considered the Monument Valley area as a focal center for the Indian peoples who first built their pit houses and then later sought shelter in their fabulous cliff palaces. Others have said that the area where the monuments reach for the sky probably contains more remains of the ancient civilization than any other area of similar size in the United States. The outstanding and remarkable thing is that only a small handful of these dwelling places have been closely examined. A few more have been seen and entered but by far the greatest number are still waiting for discovery by the white man. The trowel and camel's-hair brush of the archaeologist have rarely been felt in Monument Valley. The Indians who live there still repeat tales of great ruins located far back in the maze of canyons and mesas where no white man has ever been. When all the facts are known, it probably will be proved that suppositions and guesses were right. Monument Valley *did* provide the home for many of the Ancients— the First People.

Several remarkable cliff dwellings were discovered in the fall of 1949, when the so-called Valley of Mystery was explored for the first time. One of the first to be entered was the House of Many Hands, located at the base of a great overhanging cliff that towers seven hundred feet above. It is not properly called a cliff dwelling, for it is built on the dry sand base of the canyon floor. Only a few rooms remain standing, but indications are that this was once a great pueblo where many happy people lived.

The strangest thing about this unusual ruin is the great number of hand prints on the cliff wall. Hundreds of these prints, all different, all placed there in white paint, adorn the wall over a large surface. Was this a primitive hotel and this wall the guest register? Was it a gathering place, the town hall for the pueblo people of the valley? Or does it indicate that this pueblo was once so extensive that several hundred people lived there? The House of Many Hands still remains a mystery to be deciphered by later-day archaeologists. It gives mute answer to all questions, but it is not dead. In the full light of the moon you would expect to find ghostly shadows dancing there. For that's the way Monument Valley is. You learn to expect not only the unusual, but the ethereal as well.

Tsay-yah-kin, the House of Many People, was also discovered in late 1949. It lies in a large crevice in the side of a vast overhanging cliff at the head of a box canyon. Entrance was once gained by crossing about one hundred feet of inclined slick rock, and then using hand holds and toe holds to cover the remaining vertical distance to the cliff house. Today, these ancient hand and toe holds have been weathered away. To get into the House of Many People for the first time was a laborious task. It required several days of ladder building, precarious picking out of new hand and toe holds, and the bolting of a cable support. But, once completed, the goal was well worth the effort. The ruins, with slight change made only by the wind, were exactly as they had been when the First People left them.

There have been few white people who have gone into Tsay-yah-kin. You can count them on both hands and still have several fingers left over. It gives one a strange feeling to climb into a cliff dwelling that has remained untouched and unseen for a matter of centuries. The dust of time covers everything to the depth of many inches. And yet, beneath that dust is the charcoal of numerous fires, surrounded by tiny cobs from the corn that long ago was grown by the Ancients in the canyon and on the mesa tops.

I climbed into the House of Many People, leaving my shoes behind and going in barefooted as the First People would have done. It was an experience I shall never forget. I could feel them about me, and looking out across their canyon I could see why living there could have brought only peace of mind and the greatest of joys.

Among the twisted canyons and the great weathered domes of red rock are many other ruins, hiding away in the shadows, waiting to delight inquisitive eyes that will one day search them out and ask questions. But they will be reluctant to tell. Perhaps they will never give up the secrets of the First People in Monument Valley.

THE NAVAJOS
AND THE SPANIARDS

After the Ancient Ones came the Dine — "The People." Like all the others who came before, the Dine — a name given to themselves by the Navajo Indians — were immigrants into northern Arizona and southern Utah. They were a restless people, always on the move, never stopping long enough for a permanent home. Most authorities agree that the Navajos are descendants of the Athapascan family of Indians, most members of which live today in northwestern Canada. They roamed southward, coming into the Arizona–Utah territory about five or six hundred years ago, living from the land and foraging supplies from neighboring tribes. All of northern Arizona came to be their hunting grounds. In many ways they could be called warlike when compared to the peaceful Pueblo people who had lived there before. But their attitude was a facet of character that had been formed by a continual search for food and sustenance. They were not people of the soil. They had never acquired even the fundamentals of farming, and relied only on hunting, and raiding their neighbors. As the "have-nots" of the time they were a poor people whose meager possessions made for existence of a low scale.

The red men who lived among the great red buttes and monuments lived in a silent world of peace and contentment during the passing of many years. The tribe separated as the more warlike members went on to the south to become the present day Apaches. Only the true Navajo remained in and around Monument Valley. And he rested there undisturbed, not bothering others, while several centuries slipped by unnoticed.

To the south, the star of a mighty nation was approaching its glorious zenith. The Spain of the Old World was busy about its self-assigned job of conquering a New World. From the burning of the ships of Cortéz in the harbor of Vera Cruz, through more than three hundred years of exploration and conquest, the Spanish conquistadores and holy friars penetrated deep into a vast and unknown land that was familiar only to the red men who lived there.

Though their story is briefly and easily told, the very telling is rich in blood and pain and defeat. There was little of lasting success in the greatest portion of the Spanish explorations.

Estéban, the hulking black, whose life was already replete with adventure, crossed southern Arizona in 1539 and advanced as far as the village of Zuñi, in northern New Mexico, before he met an inglorious death at the hands of the Indians there, who did not believe his tales of being a god. Fray Marcos, who was following behind the more rapid advance of Estéban, travelled as far as the outskirts of the village, and no farther. He took one look, learned what had happened to the Negro, and hastened back to New Spain to tell about it.

Coronado followed, in 1540, with a great army of soldiers, Indians, horses, and supplies. He went first to Zuñi, where a glorious illusion was shattered when he reached this miserable Indian village, for he and his followers had believed they were approaching the fabulous golden city of Cíbola. But there was no treasure there. From that point, after the village had been appropriately subdued, Coronado sent Pedro de Tovar to investigate the Hopi, or Moqui, villages to the west, in north central Arizona. Tovar reached those villages, lingered there only briefly, then returned to Coronado's command.

Cárdenas later made the same trip via approximately the same route. He reached the Moqui villages, but rumors of a vast canyon to the west persisted, and he pushed ahead until he reached the awesome Grand Canyon of the Colorado. His point of vista probably was overlooking Glen Canyon from the site of Lee's Ferry. If this is the case, the route he followed in reaching the canyon was slightly northwestward, crossing close to more-recent Tuba City and Tonalea. But there is no definite mapping of his route and the exact point of furthest penetration cannot be correctly nor accurately defined.*

Another Spanish adventurer in search of fame and renown, Espejo, followed the footsteps of his predecessors and reached the villages of the Moqui in the early 1580's. He returned to New Mexico and Zuñi, which seemed to be the standard jumping-off place, by a more southern route through Prescott. Don Juan de Oñate was the last Spanish cavalier to enter Arizona territory. He crossed from Zuñi to the regions Espejo had explored, then traveled down the Bill Williams Fork to the Colorado River and the Gulf of California, arriving there in 1604.

So the Spanish gallants came into the land and passed away without ever having reached the valley of the monuments. They reached only as close as the Hopi villages, over one hundred miles to the south. But it is easy to see their reason for retreat before going any farther to the north. The land is desolate and forbidding. Small wonder that they turned away and investigated in other directions.

It remained for the fearless Spanish mission fathers to write the next chapter in the story. Many of these bold men of God ventured into the Arizona wilderness seeking converts and establishing missions. But, of the many, there were only three who approached to anywhere near the valley of the monuments.

On a special mission to the Hopi Indians, in 1776, Padre Francisco Tomás Garcés set out for the mysterious lands to the north. He pushed his way north along the Colorado River, finally moving eastward and reaching the present-day village of Oraibi. Oraibi was ancient even then. Established in A.D. 1200, as the cliff dwellers were leaving their northern homes and migrating to the south, Oraibi is the oldest continually inhabited town in the entire United States. Garcés stayed there for three days preaching of his Life After Death and the man named Jesus. But his gifts and golden words were rejected and he returned to San Xavier mission, completing a wilderness trip of over 2,500 miles.

On July 29, 1776, with the ink on the American Declaration of Independence scarcely dry, Father Silvestre Velez de Escalante and Father Francisco Atanasio Domingues left Santa Fe in search of a direct route to

---

* Herbert E. Bolton, in his *Coronado, Knight of Pueblos and Plains,* Albuquerque, The University of New Mexico Press, 1949, p. 139, says "The evidence indicates that it was in the vicinity of Grand View. The country was high, dry, 'open to the north,' and covered with low and twisted pines. It is at Grand View that vision sweeps north as far as Vermillion Cliffs and Lee's Ferry, some fifty miles away."—Ed.

Monterey, California, and the shores of the South Seas. They traveled first to the northwest, up through Colorado close to Utah territory. One of the eastern ruins of Hovenweep (probably Hackberry Canyon group) was passed by and scornfully commented upon in their diary. They finally entered Utah territory close to the junction of the Green River with the present-day Utah state line.

As autumn drew to a close, with the terror of winter in the high altitudes at hand, the priests were undecided as to what they should do. Some of the party believed that to return was the only salvation; others, particularly the Fathers, wished to go on. They finally drew lots to decide the question. The decision rested between continuing the search for their objective, of which thus far they had found no trace, or returning to Santa Fe by the quickest and best route they could discover. The lots fell in favor of the return to New Mexico, and the remainder of the party quickly agreed to this decision. The Virgin River was crossed near the site of St. George, Utah, and the group plunged eastward into some of the most tortuous land in the United States. For two long weeks they wandered through the badlands, finally reaching the Colorado River, and then seeking a satisfactory site for their crossing. At length, on the seventh of November, 1776, successful crossing was achieved at Padre Creek, rather than at the so-called Crossing of the Fathers, one mile to the east. They crossed approximately twenty miles to the west of Rainbow Bridge, the arch of color that was not destined to be seen by white man until over 130 years later. From that point, the party went southeast, crossing the Arizona state line at a point almost thirty miles to the west of Monument Valley. They never came close enough to the enchanted red rocks to peer down at the mystery of the monuments. Their route took the Fathers straight south to the Moqui village of Oraibi, where they turned east and southeast, finally reaching Zuñi on December 13 and Santa Fe on New Year's Day of 1777.

There is no evidence that the Navajos were ever seen by any of the Spanish explorers who came into the land during the sixteenth century. But, from the beginning of the following century, Spanish colonists were suffering from their frequent raids which continued periodically up through the middle years of the nineteenth century.

So far as we know, no Spaniard, conquistador or friar, ever entered into, or even saw, Monument Valley. But the lack of the written word is not necessarily conclusive. Perhaps in some undiscovered source in Mexico or Spain there is an account of a venture into the valley. There is a Spanish inscription dated 1640 on one of the sheer walls of Glen Canyon of the Colorado River that has never been explained. No reason has been found for it being placed there, nor is its significance clear. A local Indian legend tells of how Spanish invaders forced Indian labor to work in lead mines of the vicinity about that same period.

A mysterious Spanish inscription, generally believed to date from the 1660's, has been found in Inscription House ruin, just southwest of Monument Valley, in Navajo National Monument. And another legend has it that Montezuma escaped from his Spanish captors in Old Mexico and fled to the north, toward Arizona and Utah territory. The story relates how he was pursued and first sighted at Montezuma Creek, and later taken prisoner again at Recapture Creek. Both are streams that flow into the San Juan just northeast of Monument Valley. During the winter of 1804-1805 a Spanish expedition of soldiers entered Canyon del Muerto, near Canyon de Chelly, and staged a massacre of women and children who were hiding there.

Certainly soldiers of the empire, and men of God were abroad throughout the years of Spanish occupation in the Southwest, and just as certainly they may have entered Monument Valley.

The middle decades of the nineteenth century were a period of conflict in the western territories. The Mexican War had just been fought, and throughout northern Arizona white settlers were constantly being harassed by wary bands of Navajos. A good deal of blood was shed during those years. The result was a unique chapter in the story of Monument Valley.

In the forties and fifties, the red men were fighting a last ditch stand. They had been pushed from the shores of the Atlantic until there remained only a few isolated areas that were theirs alone. And then, never content, the white man marched on in an attempt to win all the lands of North America. The Indians fought back savagely and became desperate in their struggle. Their "warlike" nature often paled in comparison to the brutality of the whites. The Navajos watched the newcomers reach into their lands, take over the water supplies, and wipe out the wild game that once was plentiful.

The Spaniards had introduced the horse to the Navajos and it was a severe case of love at first sight—a love never staled. The horse gave the Navajo a new mobility, a new means of satisfying his restless nature. It assumed a position as the most valuable of the Navajo's few possessions. And it remains so today. A Navajo and his horse never part, and that was particularly true during the years of the Indian wars.

The United States made repeated attempts to halt the ravagings of the marauders. Treaties made in 1846, 1848, and 1849, failed to better the situation. At the basis of their failure lay an item of the greatest importance that seemed never to have entered the heads of the government peacemakers. The Navajo theory of government supported leaders only because they had the currently strong personalities and were the most capable fighters. They were leaders until someone else could take their place, and they were leaders of only small individual groups or clans. The chief from one area was not necessarily recognized by the others. Thus, when the U. S. Government believed it was signing a treaty with the Navajo nations as a whole, it was really only declaring a truce with parts of the nation. That, coupled with continued persecution by the whites, and many misunderstandings, resulted in repeated breaking of the so-called truces.

Sandstone fins in Monument Valley

PHOTOGRAPH BY GIBBS M. SMITH

The strained relations continued until 1858, with frequent expeditions being made against the Indians in the intervening years. Open warfare broke out that year when the Navajos killed a Negro servant at Fort Defiance. Another treaty followed in 1860. But attacks continued despite the new treaty and another expedition was led against the Dine. In 1860 and 1861, United States soldiers waged an active campaign, involving heavy loss of sheep and livestock by the Indians. A fifth treaty followed in 1861. Then came the crowning blow. In a dispute over a horse race at Fort Fauntleroy (near the present Fort Wingate) twelve Navajos were brutally murdered. Open warfare broke out once again and the full fury of an Indian conflict resulted.

Large numbers of United States troops had been withdrawn from the territories because of the Civil War. But with the frontier in flames something needed to be done, and done quickly. In 1863, Colonel Kit Carson was commissioned to start operations against the marauding Indians. A plan was formulated whereby all the Navajo Indians would be transferred from their reservation to the controlled restraint of the Bosque Redondo, near Fort Sumner, in New Mexico. The Indians were given the ultimatum and told to surrender by July 20 of 1863. If they did not, they would be regarded as hostile and treated accordingly. Yet, by the beginning of 1864 only two hundred Navajos had surrendered to be sent to Fort Sumner. So it was that early in that year Carson and two thousand picked men made an expedition into Canyon de Chelly to carry out what biographers called his greatest feat.

A detachment of men under Captain Albert Pfeiffer traversed Canyon del Muerto from east to west, then guarded its junction with Canyon de Chelly while Captain A. B. Carey led his men from east to west through the main gorge of that canyon. Crops and livestock were destroyed wherever found. Twenty-three Navajos, who refused to surrender, were killed, and over two hundred were captured. Thus these first Americans were taught a grisly lesson by the invading white man. By the close of 1864, over seven thousand Navajos, starved and half naked, had given themselves up and were transferred to the Bosque Redondo. By 1865, that number had increased to 8,491.

But there were some of the Navajos who were far too proud to give themselves up to captivity despite the hunger and pauperism caused by the destruction of their livestock and crops. Under the gallant leadership of the haughty Chief Hoskinnini, a small band of survivors fled to the north to escape the United States forces. Kit Carson discovered the broad trail they left behind in their hasty flight, and gave pursuit. He followed the trail all the way north to the San Juan, noting Agathlan, and passing through the valley of the monuments. When he arrived at the river he found it high with flood waters. Upon his arrival several days previously, Hoskinnini and his people had found the river in a much lower flood stage and had been successful in their crossing. And as Carson and his troopers camped on the river banks, waiting for the muddy torrent to ebb, Hoskinnini, with the craft of the Indian, recrossed the river at a safe crossing farther west. Even as Carson gave up his vigil and returned to New Mexico the people of Hoskinnini had stealthily vanished into the valley of the monuments.

Hoskinnini stayed there with his little band for the four years the others were away, at first scratching out a bare existence among the monuments. But his people gathered small flocks of sheep the soldiers had missed, and as the flocks increased, the piles of skins and wool grew.

During those years the others did not fare so well. Those who had been forced to take the fateful and awful "Long Walk" to the Bosque Redondo fought a losing battle with their environment. There, in a barren valley forty miles square, the men of the tribe were set to work digging ditches and breaking the ground for planting. But these things did not please The People. They had never been farmers and could not easily change a way of living that had been theirs for hundreds of years. They longed for their clear blue skies and haunting desert lands. More than a thousand of them died and the experiment cost the government well over a million dollars. In July of 1868, the beaten Indians who had survived were finally granted their fondest wish. All that were left, numbering 7,304, were permitted to return to their desert homeland. A government appropriation of $422,000 was made to help give them a new start.

Some of the survivors went back to their beloved Monument Valley, where they were cared for by Hoskinnini and his people. He shared with them all that he had won in the years of the imprisonment, and they called him, gratefully, the Generous One.

At the close of the imprisonment, in 1868, the Navajo Indian Reservation, largest in the United States, was established. At that time, it embraced an area of 14,333,354 acres—22,400 square miles of land, a total area much larger than the combined states of Connecticut, Rhode Island, Massachusetts, and

New Hampshire. Since that time, a section known as the Utah, or Piute, strip has been added, carrying the reservation north to the San Juan and Colorado rivers. From Crown Point, New Mexico, to the Black Falls of the Little Colorado River, just east of Wupatki National Monument, the reservation now extends for 190 miles. From Bluff, Utah, on the north, to Chambers, Arizona, on the south, the distance is 140 miles. With the addition of the Utah strip, all of Monument Valley was made official reservation of The People.

THE LEGEND
OF LOST SILVER

The Long Walk was the tragic preface to a strange and legendary chapter in the history of the valley of the monuments. It brought about a fatal rendezvous between two white men and the people of Hoskinnini, and resulted in a story that still is often repeated around campfires wherever men gather to talk of the romance and legend of the Old Southwest. It concerns a pair of reckless and foolhardy prospectors who, too late, discovered that the usual payoff in fortune hunting is disaster and sudden death.

When Colonel Kit Carson completed his military action at Canyon de Chelly and started the Indians off on their Long Walk, two men, one named Mitchell and the other named Merrick, were among the captors. It was then that they had the opportunity to notice the silver bracelets and belts that the men of the Navajo tribe wore, as well as the rings and trinkets that the women seemed to prize so greatly. The facts seemed to indicate that this wealth must have been brought from some place in the Navajo lands to the northwest, where many of these people first came from before seeking shelter in Canyon de Chelly.

As members of the government forces who patrolled the Indian country, Mitchell and Merrick knew that no silver was imported into the land by white traders or other tribes, nor where there any sources of silver money large enough to provide the metal for the wealth of beautiful silverwork that clung to the waists and wrists of these people. Somewhere to the north, the two men decided, probably in the valley of the monuments, of which they had heard vague reports, there must be a rich silver source, a mine with an inexhaustible supply of the precious metal.

With the end of the Long Walk, the two soldiers reached the end of their enlistments. They were mustered out of service, an event that fitted in perfectly with their plans. Since that first glimpse of Navajo silver they had only one thought, one dream—to find the treasure they believed was hidden to the north. And the desire drove them relentlessly to a great adventure and a fatal ending.

Assuming the guise of trappers, the two men packed into Monument Valley. Among the buttes and mesas they extended their trap lines and searched for the silver they were sure must be there. Almost immediately they encountered the Indians under the leadership of the wary Hoskinnini and were warned to return quickly whence they had come. But the lust for treasure had completely consumed these men. As with the many who came before, and the many who will come after, the thought of the precious silver drove them to risk their lives, and make a losing bet with Fate.

At length, after an extensive search, they discovered the Indian mine, and it was every bit as rich as they imagined it would be. Carefully they secured samples, concealed them within their packs, and departed from the valley. They went directly to the east, into Colorado territory, the town of Cortéz, and the nearest bar. There they told wonderful tales of the fabulous new mine they had found, the mine whose hidden location was known only to them. To substantiate their claims, they dumped their samples upon the table so that all could see. There, they said, was proof of the wealth that was already on its way into their pockets.

But before it could make them millionaires, there was one mere technicality. To extract the ore from the mine and take it into Cortéz, refine it and secure the silver, would take a lot of money. And the two prospectors were broke.

So they told and retold their tale in Cortéz and the surrounding country, going to Dolores and Mancos in the hope that somewhere they would find a man who would be willing to invest in their mine. There were many who listened to their story, but there were no takers. Several years passed and it was not until early in 1879 that a backer appeared, in the very town where they had first shown their samples.

He was Jim Jarvis, a man of the Cortéz country, who had the necessary money or knew where he could get it. From his own resources, and from a few interested friends he gathered about $4,000. With this amount he entered into an agreement with Mitchell and Merrick. He told them to go back to their hidden mine, secure more samples, and return once more to Cortéz. With new samples, to prove that the first ones were not mere chance, plus his backing, he could guarantee that additional investors would be easy to find.

The silver mine would be financed quickly, complete exploitation would follow, and in almost no time they each would have a fortune. Profits were to be split fifty-fifty, with Mitchell and Merrick retaining half interest in their mine. The original samples had been assayed at $800 to the ton. The new ones might show even a richer strike. There was a great treasure there under the red dust of the valley, and it was waiting for someone to take.

But now the venture had become even more risky. Despite every precaution the two miners had taken on that first trip into the valley, the Indians had seen them enter the mine and withdraw with the ore samplings. They did not stop the white men then, but dispatched a messenger after them with the stern warning that any man who valued his life at all would not return into the valley of the monuments. His reward would not be silver, but death.

This was no idle warning. At the time, the two men had taken it lightly and shrugged it off. But during the intervening years brief skirmishes with the Indians to the west had been of frequent occurrence. It still was the frontier; there still were Indians. Any way they looked at it now, return to the desert country seemed most dangerous. They paused, and thought twice before they took further action. But on that second thought they made their decision. They had $4,000 to back them, a partnership with a group of wealthy men, and all the pressure they had created by telling and retelling tales of bravado and courage about themselves and their hidden mine. It was no time to back down, and they returned cautiously into the valley of the monuments.

On this trip they wasted little time, and went directly to the mine. It was exactly as they had left it, and looked untouched from the last time they had been there, some years before. They cut out more of the rich ore to take back to Cortéz. And, with their hands upon more of the secret wealth, faith and the needed courage probably came quite easily. They had returned safely to the valley, gone into the mine, and still sighted no Indians. Perhaps they no longer lived in this country. After all, weren't they nomads? Now the miners had new samples—the samples that were the first step toward their wealth and fame and success. Oh, yes, this was so very easy!

But the keen eyes of the Navajo scouts, perhaps even of Hoskinnini himself, watched the two men as they entered the mine and came out with the ore samples. All right! They had been warned enough. They had been told to watch out for their lives. But white men rarely heeded the Indian. Now, let them suffer the consequences of their invasion.

Ironically enough, they waited, with the patience that is known only to the red man, until the morale and spirits of Mitchell and Merrick probably were at their zenith. They lingered until dark, when the two prospectors sat close to their fire, recounting the adventures of the day that held such golden promise. But just outside the circle of their firelight the warriors of Hoskinnini crept up in silence and suddenly were there in the firelight with the two white men. For a brief second there was a look of agonized recognition upon the faces of the two pale-faced men. Any laughter they may have been enjoying was stuck in their throats, dying and growing cold with fear. Then the tableau changed.

Merrick was killed even as he arose to his feet. Mercilessly he was shot down as a trespasser who had defied every warning. But the younger Mitchell had not yet run out of his luck. He dove back into the shadows before the Navajo warriors could finish their deathly task and send him to join his partner, now dead and lying face downward in the red dust of the valley.

Above and immediately behind them towered one of the great stone buttes that are so characteristic of Monument Valley. And this particular one became a monument to the memory of a dead man. To this day it is called Merrick Butte after the man who breathed his last in its great shadow.

Mitchell, fast though he was, was not quite fast enough. He succeeded in escaping, but not unharmed. At least one bullet found his body before he eluded his pursuers in the darkness. Painfully wounded, his only protection was the darkness that blanketed the valley. For three miles he ran and staggered across the rocks and sands. Why hadn't he listened? Why hadn't he heeded the Indian warning? But it was too late for tears. Too late for regrets. To late for everything—even life.

Finally he reached the sloping base of another butte and hid there among the red rocks that had scaled from the sheer walls above and tumbled down the talus slopes. He waited there among the rocks until sunrise. Then the Indians found him, waited until he had exhausted all his ammunition, and crept in and killed him as they had Merrick. To commemorate his adventure there is another monument—another tombstone that reached skyward in those first rays of a new dawn. It is Mitchell Butte, that stands at the head of Mitchell Butte Wash in Monument Valley, silent testimony of the drama that was staged there.

Far away, in Cortéz and Mancos, those men who had already invested their savings in the Mitchell-Merrick interests were hungering for the return of the two miners and were concerned about their long delay. Then came a strange rumor from out of the valley, and, fearful that it might be true, they formed a posse and headed west for Monument Valley through McElmo Canyon and across Sage Plain. They were twenty-two in number, a group large enough to protect themselves from the Indian marauders.

When they reached the valley and had searched the area, their worst

Merrick Butte, framed by a weathered juniper

PHOTOGRAPH BY ROBERT Z. BRUCKMAN

Mystery Valley
PHOTOGRAPH BY GIBBS M. SMITH

fears were confirmed. When questioned, the Navajos led the posse members to two recent graves. And buried in these two shallow graves, covered with the red rock of the valley, were the bodies of the fortune-hunters. On the body of Mitchell they found the last rich ore samples that had been taken from the mine. But there was nothing else.

The Navajos who had helped to find the bodies said a renegade band of Piutes had committed the crime. This is the story they told: Mitchell and Merrick had stopped one morning at the hogan of Hoskinnini and had demanded mutton. After it had been killed for them, they were directed to water. When they had filled their canteens and watered their horses, the two prospectors camped at the base of Merrick Butte.

In the morning, as the white men were preparing to move on, a band of Piutes who had been planning a surprise attack came into the prospectors' camp and found them already mounted. The Indians claimed the white men had been using Piute water to which they had no right. Both men answered calmly that they had been sent to the water by Chief Hoskinnini. Despite various attempts to pick a quarrel and irritate the two whites into a fight, the Indians were not successful. One Piute turned to Merrick and demanded a chew of tobacco. As the prospector reached into his pocket, the Indian reached for Merrick's gun. A moment later Merrick was lying on the ground—killed with a bullet from his own rifle.

Mitchell got away to Mitchell Butte, where he was wounded while hiding among the rocks. The Piutes left him there and he died of starvation and his wounds at the base of the towering butte.

That was the story. But to the men of the posse there was a better one. It was the one that explained why two men who had been hunting for Navajo silver and had been twice warned by a Navajo chieftain had met death in a Navajo valley. But they didn't argue with Hoskinnini.

The secret of the hidden mine was as well-kept as ever. There were no clues to its location, no hint or suggestion of any kind that helped to lift the curtain of surrounding mystery. The posse reburied the bodies, made vague attempts at locating the mine, then left the country in early 1881 and went back to Colorado.

The fate of Mitchell and Merrick soon became legendary. The story of their rich Navajo silver mine was told wherever men gathered to listen. A few of them ventured into the place of the monuments with the shining hope that it would be they who rediscovered the great silver source. But now the task of discovery had grown much greater. Fearful lest many more white men come into their country and search for the silver, the Navajo tribal leaders met in secret council and decided that their mine should be closed forever. They covered the only entrance with rock and sand and hid it from the inquisitive world. As long as those twelve leaders lived, the secret would live too. But with their passing, the secret could never be told.

A few years passed by unnoticed, as so many thousand already have there in Monument Valley. Then it was that a man named Cass Hite played his role in the story of the lost silver mine and the history of the valley of the monuments. A supposed renegade, and a one-time member of Quantrill's Civil War guerrillas, Hite had come into the Escalante country of Utah in the early 1870's. He had settled on the Colorado River at a place that still bears his name—Hite. He built a rock hovel there, at one of the few places the mighty Colorado could be crossed with any assurance of safety. He had the country pretty much to himself and lived his life as he wanted it.

In 1893, a group of prospectors came to Hite and asked him about gold in that country. Whether he believed it himself, or whether he merely wanted to get rid of them, he gave them a good story. He told of how coarse gold had washed down to the riffles and sandbars at the foot of Navajo Mountain.

The prospectors, typically hungry for sudden wealth, swallowed his story. They went south, made sample pannings, and sure enough, there was gold! True, it was fine, but there must be more. The rush was on. Ferries were built and great dredges were hauled in laboriously through almost impassably rough country to the muddy Rio Colorado. Today, these machines lie twisted and rusted, silent under a burning sun. For there was no wealth of gold there. It was powder-fine, like flour, and assayed at only a few dollars to the ton. The cost of operation could not possibly be paid for. Disappointed and revenge-seeking, the prospectors went after Cass Hite, intending to have his hide. But the resourceful isolationist decided that

Merrick Butte and the Mittens
PHOTOGRAPH BY ROBERT Z. BRUCKMAN

this was the very moment when he should leave the country and try something else he had been intending to do for a number of years.

He had heard tales of the lost Navajo mine in Monument Valley and had decided that he knew of a way that it could be found. Carefully avoiding the camps of the irate miners, he escaped to the south, into the valley. For some reason the people of Hoskinnini took a liking to this lone white man. He lived there among them for two years, gaining their confidence and friendship. He was sure they knew the secret of the mine's location, these simple people who had no real use for their silver. And he was sure also that in time he could extract their secret from them and find the mine for himself.

Strangely, his ruse worked—up to a point. The family he lived with took him to their hearts. They believed his wise words. When he told them that they had everything to gain and nothing to lose by opening the mine for him and sharing in its wealth, his eloquence convinced the leader of the family, who was one of the original tribesmen who had buried the mine.

But, successful as his plan seemed to be, Cass Hite had forgotten to reckon with one thing. He had forgotten Hoskinnini, the crafty chief who seemed to have eyes in the back of his head, and who always learned of any plot that was planned among his people. He found out about Hite's intention to reopen the mine. Around a campfire, he told the others of his tribe. And, when told, they rose up against the white man and the people with whom he lived. That family and their friend were threatened, but Hite acted quickly and saved the day. His luck was better than that of his predecessors, probably only because he had not gone as far. He quietly disappeared from the valley and returned to the north, where bad feeling had finally subsided and it was safe to go once more. Cass Hite never returned to Monument Valley. He knew better!

But a rich treasure never remains hidden and unsought for. There have been many who have packed into the valley, or even driven in, but their luck has been no better than the ones who came before. The tale has become legendary even among the Indians, and probably none of the tribe knows the secret location of the mine. It is as much a mystery to the Navajo as it is to the white man. Or is it?

Evidently the mine is an isolated strike, a peculiarity in this country that abounds in peculiarities. Some say that if it is to be found at all, it will be found in the igneous rock that dots the valley floor. For they say that only in rock of volcanic origin, that has been thrust up from deep in the earth, could silver be found. Perhaps so, perhaps not. Either way, it has never been found. Nor have any other sources of silver ore ever been discovered in the valley, despite all the extensive searches that have been undertaken.

Though Mitchell and Merrick were camped in the central part of the valley when their Red Fate consumed them, that fact alone does not mean that the mine is located close by. Doubtless the Indians delayed their attack, waiting for the two men to leave the mine far behind. But wherever the mine is, it has been undisturbed for almost eighty years. In the shade of the great god-like mesas and buttes of Monument Valley the Mitchell-Merrick mine smiles and yawns, then sleeps without concern.

THE PLACE
OF MOONLIGHT WATER

From far to the east came the first white people, two families, the descendants of which were destined to make a part of Monument Valley their home. They joined the nomads in their land of room enough and time enough, and they learned to love it even as the red man does.

From Pennsylvania came the Quaker named Benjamin Kite Wetherill, by profession a peacemaker, an occupation that befitted his religion. He rode the Chisholm Trail, doing his part to smooth the troubled relations with the plains tribes in those days of the closing frontier. In the six years from 1870 to 1876 he continued these duties of arbitration, leaving his wife behind in Leavenworth. Then, in 1876, they moved to Joplin, Missouri, where he leased a mine.

The Wetherills lived in Joplin until 1879, when failing health combined with the necessity for a new occupation and drove the peacemaker westward alone. His great desire to go west was fanned into flame by the restlessness that had created an empire. For over two hundred years, hundreds of men and women had been swept up by this wave of enthusiasm and carried toward the Pacific, to carve out the new frontier. Colorado had just achieved statehood, but the surge westward had reached its peak. The spark was dying and the wave gradually lost its momentum. Still the lands beyond the horizon beckoned and called. It was a part of a man's country, to be fought for and won, to be settled for a man and his family. So Ben Wetherill went westward until he reached the mines at Rico, Colorado, and he stopped there.

In Virginia, another family started its wanderings. Uprooted by the Civil War, the Wades migrated into Iowa. For awhile they were happy there, then the call sounded and to the west with the restless people went young Jack Wade with his father and family. In Nevada, he found a wife for himself, a woman of the heroic blood that permeated the frontier and made it strong. Her father, James Martin Rush, was a fiery man, famous all along the frontier for his quick courage. He had been a Texas Ranger, one of the first to ride along the Chisholm Trail; he had fought in the Mexican War, and with the Confederate Army during the Civil War. In Jack Wade he found a son-in-law after his own heart, and from that time on they rode the lonely trails together. In Nevada, Jack Wade turned to mining and moved with his wife from camp to camp during the exciting days of the Comstock Lode. In the mining camps, their first two children, Jim and Louisa, were born. And from the Nevada mining camps Jack and Martin moved again, this time, in the year 1879, bound for the mining camps of Colorado, looking for another new home.

Wade and Rush, riding together as usual, ran into renegade Utes near Dolores, Colorado, and realized the great dangers that the country held. They somehow escaped safely from the red men, but learned a few days later that the same war party had completely wiped out the government agency, killing the agent and his employees, and taking his wife and children as captives. Going on farther, Wade and Rush joined a party of cowpunchers from the Mancos Valley to go after the Indians. After a few days, when they returned into the fertile valley of the Mancos River, they realized at once that this must be home.

Rush stayed in the valley to plant the crops and build a home. Jack Wade went on alone to bring back his wife and family. But before leaving Colorado he talked with a grizzled miner, named Merrick, who had brought silver ore samples from the Navajo country, assaying $800 to the ton. He was intrigued, but pushed on to Nevada. It was Wade's first touch with the land that was one day to be the home of his daughter.

Even as B. K. Wetherill sent back to Missouri for his family to come to Rico, a wagon train set out for the Mancos Valley from Dutch Creek,

Nevada. That was in the late fall of 1879. In that wagon train was Jim Wade, four years old, Louisa, two years old, and George, still in his mother's arms. Three children, two women (mother and grandmother), and a man, setting forth into an unknown country with the faith and courage of the dauntless pioneer.

There was bad luck even from the first. Snow in the Wasatch Mountains, forced the party to detour by the longer southern route. The community of Silver Reef was finally reached on Christmas Day, and the party delayed there while Jack Wade timbered a mine. Then, with additional supplies, they moved on to their destination in the Mancos Valley. They crossed the Colorado River at Lee's Ferry, heading across new and strange lands toward Moenkopi, the Mormon settlement to the southeast.

At Moenkopi they were warned of the dangerous country that was ahead. They heard the ominous rumor of the tragic fate of the two miners, Mitchell and Merrick. That tale recalled to Jack Wade the memory of the old miner he had talked with back in Colorado, and he remembered his hesitation at going along on the prospecting trip. Merrick and his friend Mitchell had come face to face with their executioners in the very land that the Wades were now heading for. But now there was no turning back.

They headed northeast from Moenkopi, across the loose sands toward Red Lake (Tonalea) and up the wash that took them toward Kaibito. They had no map, but, at last, realized they must be off their planned route. The load was lightened as chinaware and other last ties with home were buried in the sands of White Mesa Wash. Then they turned toward Marsh Pass, where they camped at the base of Tsegi* Mesa. The following night they camped near the spring at Todanestya (Kayenta). From this place, "Where Water Comes out Like Fingers From a Hill," the wagons crept on across the desolate lands to the east. The great buttes of Monument Valley were just to the north, hidden only by the toothlike Comb Ridge. Supplies again ran low, and on one occasion they had to dig into the burning sands to find water. Only beans remained for rations, and they were gritty with sand. But finally the caravan crept into the San Juan Valley, where the Wades were able to purchase salt pork and molasses. On May 19, 1880, they went into the Mancos Valley and found home.

Martin Rush had been busy while they were gone. He told of how he,

* Most official maps give spelling as "Segi."—Ed.

too, had talked with Merrick and had been urged to go on the trip into Monument Valley. But he decided to remain behind with the crops, waiting for Wade and his family.

The memory of the rich ore samples he had seen intrigued Jack Wade into joining the twenty-two-man posse which rode into Monument Valley in search of Merrick and Mitchell late in 1880. On Christmas day, 1880, Wade wrote to his wife from the foot of the great black shaft that was called El Capitan by Kit Carson when he passed there in pursuit of Hos-kinnini, and Agathlan, "The Place of the Scraping of the Hides," by the Navajos. In the following days, they examined the territory around Oljeto, the "Place of the Moonlight Water." Then, in February 1881, they returned to Mancos and told the people there of the things they had seen—sweeping sands, the high red cliffs, El Capitan, and Oljeto.

In June of 1881, the Wetherills arrived in Rico and were united with their father and husband. They moved on west and farmed for awhile at Bluff, Utah, but that first ranch was washed out by the desert rains and they abandoned it. In the Mancos Valley they acquired about a thousand acres of land and made a new attempt.

Though the years passed, Jack Wade could never forget the silver ore samples he had seen nor the wonderful tales of the rich Mitchell and Merrick mine. At one time he grubstaked an old prospector who was planning to venture into the valley of the monuments. But the prospector promptly drank up all the money. At the end of his bender, he returned to Wade and asked for more money, but was refused. Finally, to the accompanying jeers of the townspeople, he set off in his old buggy with only a pie and a buggy whip. Later, he sent back word he had discovered a mountain of copper and needed $50 to stake his claim. Again Wade refused him. The mine the old man found later turned out to be the fabulous Copper Queen, and Jack Wade had lost out on a fortune.

It was in Mancos that the winding trails of the Wetherills and the Wades finally came together. Louisa Wade and John Wetherill met, romanced, and later were married on March 17, 1896, in Mancos, the tiny town huddled in the shade of La Plata Mountains, from whose slopes one could look far into the desert country, and, on a clear day, even see the buttes and pinnacles of Monument Valley. And that land came to be a part of the romance of the Wetherills' life. They listened and eagerly drank in every tale of the land of the monuments to the southwest. Whenever occasion presented itself, John Wetherill acted as guide for scientific parties that went into the land of the Navajos. And when he returned he was always full of wonderful stories for Louisa.

He went often on these trips and became known as a trusted and reliable guide. That reputation was further enhanced by his discoveries of ruins in the dry canyons of the Mesa Verde. It was said that John Wetherill, more than any other man of that country, knew the difficult trails and the location of every hidden water hole and seep, all-important there in the land of little water. He knew the canyons where ancient cliff ruins still held secrets, and he came to be accepted as a personal friend by the red peoples of the desert.

Louisa and John Wetherill moved to Ojo Alamo in December of 1900. Jack Wade visited them there, and, still filled with the wondrous stories of the Mitchell and Merrick mine, he decided to make one more attempt at locating the site. He described a large intrusive body of ore he had found near Oljeto in 1892. It might hold silver, and he was determined to find out. John Wetherill and Jack Wade set out for Oljeto in 1901. They did not find the intrusion, but never gave up hope. "We'll try again."

And they did try again. Late that same year they once again packed into the place of the monuments, this time with three companions. They found the igneous rock on this attempt, but there was no trace of the silver there. The Mitchell and Merrick mine still remained hidden.

On a sunny day in February, 1906, John Wetherill, Jack Wade, and Clyde Colville set out to look for a new home. Unrest was still biting at their heels and in the final death throes of the frontier they set out to find a place that would retain some of the taste of the old days. They came up from Farmington, New Mexico, to Mancos and Cortéz, then wandered west to the San Juan. At Moses Rock, southeast of Mexican Hat, they left Colville with a part of the load, when one of their wagons broke down.

Wetherill and Wade continued on into Monument Valley to find again the "Place of the Moonlight Water." Between the great buttes of the valley of the monuments, where he had first come as a prospector, John Wetherill now came as a trader to find a place where he could make his home. On March 17, 1906, the two men rode at last to the "Place of the Moonlight Water"—to the cottonwoods and high red mesas—to Oljeto.

They were met there by the tall and thin grey-haired son of Hoskinnini. Without ceremony he told the white men to leave the land. But they stood their ground despite the warnings of Hoskinnini-begay. Wade went back for Colville and the remainder of the supplies, leaving Wetherill alone in an alien land. But though he was alone, he talked with the Indians and won them over to his side. His first suggestion was that a feast be held, so that they might carefully consider the idea of his staying in the valley. He promised to provide flour, sugar, and coffee, if the Indians would bring the rabbits. The people of Hoskinnini agreed, and in three days they gathered for a feast.

From sunrise to sunset, Wetherill talked with the people. "I've never had any reason for using a gun," he told them. "I have never had to fight my way into any country. Always I have come as a friend."

He pointed out the many obvious advantages that would be realized if a trading post was set up in their land. They could buy flour, sugar, salt, and coffee whenever they needed it, and they could pawn or sell silver

Early auto touring in Monument Valley
PHOTOGRAPHER UNKNOWN

and turquoise. It was far to the other trading posts. Many miles of hard riding over the arid high country. Round Rock was ninety miles to the west. It was seventy miles to Red Lake and eighty to Bluff. It was a long way to ride for flour to cook the kind of bread they were eating now.

They nodded their heads and agreed with his words. At length, after great deliberation, Hoskinnini and Hoskinnini-begay told Wetherill that he could stay in the "Place of the Moonlight Water." When Wade and Colville came with the supplies, John Wetherill returned to Pueblo Bonito, where he had left his wife, and brought her back to Monument Valley with him. Within twenty days they arrived at Oljeto.

That first night in the "Place of the Moonlight Water," they stood together before the tents which were to be their home and place of business for months to come, until they had built a permanent home. They looked out over that wonderful land they had dreamed of for so long. The high red mesas stood on three sides, touched with the silver light of the moon, and threw long shadows that seemed to bridge time and space from their world into eternity. To the north stood the Henry Mountains, rose at dusk, then deepening to purple, and finally to black silhouettes as the night came on. Now this was their land, and they felt rich for being there. As leased government traders, they belonged to the land.

In that first week one of the men went after additional supplies to Gallup, while in Oljeto they moved their tents nearer to the Moonlight Water, laid a board across two coffee boxes and made ready to trade. With the help of the now-friendly Navajos they soon began to build a home. But the work advanced at the leisurely pace of the high desert lands, and their home took shape slowly.

In 1908, there came news that a party of United States soldiers was marching toward Oljeto from the east. The people of Hoskinnini grew afraid as they suddenly felt a resurgence of their old fear for the white man. They did not like the idea of what approaching troops might mean. Only two years before, in the Four Corners country, a slight skirmish had taken place, resulting in several dead Navajos as well as a number of Army fatalities. A band of Navajos, suddenly coming upon a large group of soldiers, had mistaken their intent, and fired into them. Even as they did, the troops, still nervous and uncertain about Indian relations, and very doubtful as to the friendship of a large band of Indians that suddenly appeared on the horizon, fired back. The mutual misunderstanding had resulted in a feeling of resentment among the Indians. Now as the people of Monument Valley heard of a new army approaching their lands, they were afraid. Too well, many of them still remembered the Long Walk.

It remained for Louisa Wetherill to talk with the gallant Hoskinnini and urge him to send a message of peace and friendship to the United States troops. He accepted her advice, and went to the east as far as Laguna Wash, which he discovered to be in flood. He waited there for three days, while the government forces approached and waited on the other side. At length Hoskinnini, tired of his wait, tied the message to a rock and threw it across the flood waters, returning then to Oljeto.

The soldiers, under the leadership of Colonel Hunter, actually numbered six hundred and were out on a mission to capture a number of renegade Indians who repeatedly had been causing trouble. They succeeded finally

Navajo woman weaving, ca. 1947

PHOTOGRAPH BY WALT TREADWELL

in crossing the wash and went on west to Oljeto. There they were greeted by the silent but peaceful Indians. A council fire was agreed upon so that common grievances could be aired.

At first the Indians were sullen and afraid, but as Colonel Hunter explained his mission The People understood. He had come to take renegade Indians as prisoners, but at Oljeto there was only peace. They had nothing to fear. Before, the Indians had killed because they feared the white man. But then the Wetherills had come into the land and brought friendship. Now there was only peace. Around the council fire the Indians were told that they would soon be given schools and plows, as well as their many other needs. Then the soldiers left, taking no prisoners with them.

Hoskinnini, the last great chief of the Navajos, died on October 31, 1909. His last request was that he might talk with Louisa Wetherill, whom he called and considered his granddaughter. But by the time she had been told of his request, and had gone the many miles to see him, he had already passed away to his happiest of hunting grounds. What he wished to tell her will always remain unknown. He held a definite affection for his white "granddaughter" and it is certain he wished to give her a portion of his lands. But there was something else, something he refused to confide even to those about him when he died. Some say he wished to give her a sack of precious stones, while others say that he wished to tell her the secret of the Mitchell and Merrick mine. Whatever his last wish was, it remained unexpressed.

The People dressed their chieftain in his best robes so that the spirits of the underworld might know at once that this was a good man who had lived justly and generously, and who had many friends to prepare him for his last journey. If they had dressed him in rags, the spirits would think he had lost all his friends, been unjust, and gambled away his goods. They put his moccasins on the wrong feet so that the spirit of the chief might not make tracks like a living person. Then the burial party, dressed only in loincloths, let their hair fall about their shoulders, and painted their bodies with ashes and soot from burned ceremonial plants. This was the custom when a person died a natural death.

The hogan of the proud Hoskinnini was burned and his family sat there beside it with blankets over their heads. The three members of the burial party saddled and bridled the chief's favorite horse and put the body of its owner across the saddle. As one led the way, the other two held the body and they went to the place of the burial. They built a small hogan of poles under rocks, and placed him there. With him, they placed his saddle, his bridle, bit and ropes. The saddle was broken, the bridle and ropes cut, and the bit mashed with stones. They broke all his beads, and made tears in his robes so that the thought that had gone into the making of all these things might go with the spirit of the chief. For nothing really dies. It is only lent by Mother Earth for a brief period of use. Then it must go back from whence it came, to the land of peace and summer, where it continues to live on forever. Even the thought that went into the making of his possessions would go back. For the thought comes from the Great Spirit and is to be treasured. Certainly there is a bit of Indian philosophy that stands out as something pure and noble.

When all the ceremonies had been completed, the grave was closed. Then his horse was stoned and killed, so that the spirit of Hoskinnini might always ride it. And I'm certain, as you will be too when you have seen the valley of the monuments at twilight, that the spirit of the Generous One, Hoskinnini, rides there still.

Indian ponies crossing the Valley
PHOTOGRAPH BY RONALD W. HARRIS

Four days of mourning followed. The three men of the burial team stood close guard over the trail that went to the burial place, for nothing must cross that trail. The people remembered their great chief and spoke of his many good deeds. They recalled tales of how he outwitted Kit Carson, and brought his people safely into the valley of the monuments. And they remembered how he had gathered stray sheep and goats, and how he had fed with a generous hand the people who had finally returned from the Bosque Redondo. Though he was old when he left them for his underworld journey, it was only his body which was old. The spirit is always one of a person in the prime of life.

When the four days had ended, it was Louisa Wetherill who divided the property of the great chief. She divided it equally and justly, and though they asked her to keep more for herself, she kept only the chief's gun as her share.

In 1909, a suspension bridge was built across the San Juan at Mexican Hat (then Goodridge). A bridge at the Hat meant removal of a water barrier that had kept Oljeto shut off from the rest of the world. In fact, it meant final removal of an obstacle that had acted as a barricade to Monument Valley all through the hundreds of years when white men, Spanish and American, had circled and edged the area of the monuments. A great desert on three sides and a river to the north had guarded their prized valley well, allowing only a chosen few to see it. Now, the building of a bridge was somehow the end of an age. It meant that there was new contact with the world that was outside. It was an event well-received at Oljeto.

The trading post at the "Place of the Moonlight Water" soon became headquarters for adventure-seekers who wanted to go in to the Rainbow Bridge, discovered in 1909 and designated a National Monument by President Theodore Roosevelt on May 30, 1910. Less than two months after it was said that no woman would ever be able to endure the hazardous trail that went in to the bridge from Oljeto, the first woman came to the trading post and successfully made the trip. The pioneer stock of the early days had not yet vanished.

But though the San Juan had been bridged, the Wetherills were still seventy miles from their nearest white neighbor. And supplies still had to be freighted in from Gallup across 190 miles of sand or mud and arroyos that presented formidable hazards at all seasons of the year. Holidays especially were cherished. One summer John Wetherill rode the 190 miles to Gallup, and back, in four days for fireworks for the Fourth of July. On Christmas, there was always a present for everyone—family members and Indians alike. Slow delivery and great delays meant that presents must be ordered far ahead because of the uncertainty of arrival. One year presents that were ordered in August arrived, only slightly delayed, the following August.

In 1910, the Wetherills moved to the place known as Todanestya, where they still were farther from a railroad than any other white settlement in the United States. For awhile they called their new home Oljeto, then it was called Kayenta, for the deep spring located three miles away. Teddy Roosevelt came there in 1912, and stayed at the Wetherill ranch, later going on to see the wonder of Rainbow Bridge. His publicizing of the area brought a new kind of person into the land—the tourist.

The Wetherills remained at Kayenta for the rest of their days although John Wetherill served as custodian of nearby Navajo National Monument for a number of years. In November of 1944 he made his last great journey, and, appropriately enough, his wife soon followed him as she always had throughout their rich, full life. With their departure from the place of the monuments, a noble chapter in its history had come to a close.

OUTLAW TRAILS

During the years that closed one century and gave birth to a new one, there were others who came into Monument Valley from time to time. But they did not come to enjoy the scenery, and they rarely stayed for long. Among those who came there again and again, for only a single campfire, or a few days at most, were members of the fabled Robber's Roost gang, the Wild Bunch that terrorized the West from Canada to Mexico and from Nebraska to the Pacific coast between 1870 and 1904. While the frontier lived, they lived too. And as it faded, so did they.

Of those who have followed the Outlaw Trail, there are few more fabulous than Butch Cassidy, a leader of the Wild Bunch. With detail and precision, he carefully planned each of his renowned escapades. Born as LeRoy Parker, of Mormon parents, in Circleville, Utah, Butch Cassidy was in performance somewhat of a Western Robin Hood. He started his infamous career as a bank and payroll robber, but then turned to cattle rustling in later years. Anyone who found himself in need could always go to Cassidy for help. If the colorful outlaw didn't have the money, he knew of someone who could stand to part with some, and went about the task of getting it. He seemed to carry out his banditry for the mere enjoyment of the adventure and excitement that it brought to him. In all his years of riding Western trails, and in all his variety of exploits, Cassidy was never known to have killed a man.

The Robber's Roost, which was generally central headquarters for Butch Cassidy and his Wild Bunch, was located in the heart of the San Rafael Swell, in Utah. But they used various other locales as headquarters from year to year. Hanksville was used extensively in the eighties and nineties as a rendezvous point for the gang. From there they often crossed the Colorado at Hite's river crossing and proceeded south to the Four Corners country. That territory was a favorite haunt because it made pursuit so difficult. Let a sheriff from Utah follow them with a warrant, and they slipped unconcerned into any one of the three other states that were there to choose from. An endless game could follow, and the law always tired first.

The gang passed through Monument Valley often, as did others of the outlaw kingdom, on their way to points south. They knew of every water-hole and seep, and found traveling in the dry lands to be no particular hazard. They loved their wild existence and lived it to the hilt. They passed through so quickly that they were not bothered by the Indians, nor in their brief passage did they bother the Navajos.

But their era passed with the coming of a new century and the gasping breaths of the dying frontier. The gang broke up in the early 1900's. Cassidy disappeared, supposedly to South America to start a cattle ranch there. Rumor reported he was killed there some years later. What actually became of him no one really knows. Probably his spirit is one of the many that linger and ride by moonlight among the monuments.

MORMONS AND MINERS

The story of Monument Valley would not be complete if it left untold the portion written by the Mormons, the hardy pioneers who had already played the all-important role of colonizing of Utah. Almost every part of that state had been penetrated and Mormon-settled. Even northern Arizona was included in the zealous efforts made by the Saints to establish their planned state of Deseret, and though the nature of the country made the art of settlement most difficult, their determination never once lessened, and every challenge was met.

Tuba City was only one of their many far-flung settlements. The village that was later to become capital of the Western Navajo Indian nations was laid out in 1878 as an outgrowth of the mission at nearby Moenkopi, which had been established by the Mormon fathers seven years earlier, in 1871. Even today, though its reign as Indian capital has passed, Tuba remains one of the more important villages in Navajo land.

The year following the founding of that city, an exploration party under the capable direction and able leadership of Silas S. Smith set out from Cedar City, Utah, to make a detailed study of the land in the San Juan Valley. Approaching waves of settlers from the East left that valley in imminent danger of settlement by Gentiles, something that could not be allowed to happen. The expedition left Cedar City in 1879 and travelled

southward, crossed the Colorado River at Lee's Ferry and continued on
to Tuba City. From there, they turned north. They passed close to the
valley of the monuments, reached the San Juan and established a fort at
the mouth of Montezuma Creek. Leaving several families behind, to stay
with the land, the remainder of the exploration party continued north and
returned eventually to Cedar City. Immediately upon their arrival, when
the church had learned details of the expedition, a call was sent out for
two hundred members of the church to settle in the San Juan country.
With true church patriotism, the number called for responded, and prepared

Sandstone tapestry, Monument Valley

PHOTOGRAPH BY ROBERT Z. BRUCKMAN

for one of the most outstanding episodes in the entire history of our frontier.

The route followed by Smith and his party was immediately concluded to be too circuitous, and a route going directly to the destination was decided upon. With little more than a scant look into the records that told, with emphasis, of the desolate country they were going to pass through, they jumped off into the wilderness in December, 1879. The barrier they attempted to cross was almost insurmountable. But they took it in their determined stride. For better than four months they fought their way across several hundred miles of wilds that, even today, remain relatively untouched and unconquered. They crossed the Colorado at the Hole in the Rock, where it is difficult to cross safely with a horse, let alone a wagon train, and arrived at Montezuma Creek in April of 1880.

The town of Bluff was established and boasted of a population of 225 inhabitants. But during that first year, almost half of the population gave up and moved away. Trouble with the Indians, constant adverse weather, and unsuccessful attempts at irrigation finally caused even the ambitious Mormons to pack up and move north.

For two decades the half-deserted town remained the end of the line. There was no road south into Monument Valley. It was strictly foot and horseback country, even as it is, largely, today. Discovery of gold in the upper tributaries of the San Juan had caused E. L. Goodridge to make the first known boat trip down the San Juan in 1879. He found very little in the way of gold dust, but he found something else that surprised and interested him more. Just north of Monument Valley, on the banks of the San Juan, he found oil seeps coming from beneath loose boulders. He sought the necessary funds to exploit his discovery, and, finally, in 1907, succeeded in drilling a well and uncorked a gusher "throwing oil to the height of seventy feet." There followed a rush to file claims in the area, and, by 1911, the road had been extended down from Bluff. That year there were twenty-seven drilling rigs in the field, but most of them produced only a little oil or gas, and many were dry holes. None of them paid off commercially.

During the year 1891, almost two thousand miners came into the country, lured by the oft-repeated tales of gold strikes that were being told in the East. A few of the men succeeded in making expenses from the flour-like gold they found, but the rest drifted on to the blue Abajos, or were among those who questioned Cass Hite about gold on the Colorado and pushed to the southwest, only to succumb to a second disappointment.

James Douglas discovered gold in a San Juan sandbar in 1909, when the river was at an unusually low stage. But before he could file his claim and get back to extract the gold, the river rose to its normal height and hid it from him. For twenty years he waited patiently for the river to go down again. Finally he gave up, in 1929, and committed suicide from the bridge at Mexican Hat. Five years later, the river, with its ironical sense of humor, went stone dry.

Even though the age-old quest for gold, and the relatively new search for black gold was carried on within sight of the valley of the monuments, it suffered or benefited little from the neighboring exploitation. Until 1921 only one automobile had crossed the bridge at the Hat. The valley remained alone and waited for the friend it knew would come soon.

KING AND QUEEN
OF THE VALLEY

The friend and champion came in
the summer of 1921, when a young sheepherder gently urged his horse up
the desolate eastern slope of Comb Ridge. As he topped the ridge, he sat up
tall in the saddle, pushed back his hat, and looked to the west. There it was.
The land he had dreamed of. He saw the valley of the monuments sprawled
out before him. With all its glorious color and its striking magnificence it
made a breath-taking and inspiring sight to the young man from Colorado.

That was Harry Goulding's first introduction to the valley of the monuments, and although there was no one there to assist in the introduction,
it was clearly a case of love at first sight. He was on a journey that aptly
combined business with pleasure. Riding the Four Corners country looking
for stray sheep, he happened into the valley more or less by chance. But not
completely. He had been looking for a home ever since his discharge from
the army after World War I and rode west on purpose, though he knew
there would be no strays there. It was one of those cases that seem
predestined to have worked out as neatly as it did. Since that first chance
meeting the valley and the man have been inseparable. With his first
glimpse of the red buttes and mesas, Harry Goulding knew deep inside
that this somehow must belong to him and become his home. But it seemed
only a dream—far from reality. Monument Valley then was included in

the Piute Indian Reservation which made private ownership impossible. So Harry returned home, to wait and continue his dream for another year.

The picture changed within little more than that single year. In 1923, the Utah legislature offered the Piute tribes a section of more fertile land to the north, and the Indians accepted. As a result, the former reservation reverted to public domain and was opened for homesteading. It was the chance of a lifetime and it came when Harry Goulding wanted it most. He hesitated only long enough to help his young wife pack their belongings, and they were off for Monument Valley.

"Mike" Goulding acquired her nickname back in the days when Harry was courting her in Colorado. Her real name is Leone, but that's a hard name to spell when you've only had one year of high-school education. For Harry it came out a different way every time, and never the right way. He argued with it for several letters, then came the showdown. "Ma'm . . .

The trading post was used as a movie set in the 1948 film *She Wore a Yellow Ribbon*
PHOTOGRAPH BY ALEX KAHLE

your name is going to be Mike from now on!" He could spell Mike. And that's the way it stands today. It's always "Mike," the queen of Monument Valley.

The Goulding caravan, as it came into the valley, must have been a real sight to behold. Especially to the red man, who would never have believed that it could happen in his land. Harry came first, over the old "road" that ran to the east of the present road. It had never seen a road grader, in fact, it hadn't even seen many cars. He was driving a one-and-a-half-ton Graham Brothers truck, armed with a special auxiliary transmission—ten gears forward. And through the red sand and loose rock, Harry used every one of those ten gears. Behind him, to complete the spectacle, and fighting with that same sand and rock, came Mike, driving a great lumbering 1922 soft-topped Buick, carrying 1,400 pounds of load. It had over-sized tires, something they were soon to grow used to in Monument Valley. Large tires were better at conquering the red dust.

Harry laid claim to 640 acres of Monument Valley, at the base of Tsay-Kizzi Mesa, the Big Rock Door Mesa, as the Indians called it. The square mile cost him $320. For every dollar he invested he received two acres of the most enchanted land in all the world. A part of Monument Valley was actually his own. In a little more than a year after that precious moment when he had first seen the valley, he returned and really did hang his hat on "a place to call home" as he had said he would do on that first glorious viewing of the place of the monuments.

Harry had both practical and romantic reasons for coming to the valley of the red monuments. Basic to all was his desire to get away from civilization. He came with a few sheep, planning to run stock in the valley as he had back home, and he came as a licensed trader, hoping to set up a post and trade with the Indians. And he had a thought to the future that gave further reason for coming into the valley. Harry believed that some day people from all over the world would be visiting Monument Valley to see its wonders. And when they came, he wanted to be there to show it to them.

He set up the tents and prepared to stay awhile. He chose the place at the base of the Big Rock Door Mesa for a number of reason. The sheer, eight-hundred-foot, slick-rock cliff provided good protection from wind and heat at all times of the year. And the view from his site was outstanding. You can realize that today when you visit Harry Goulding's Monument Valley Trading Post and Lodge. The view from his front porch outmatches anything to be seen anywhere in the world. It's awesome, fabulous, and remarkable. Looking straight ahead you can see for sixty-five miles, turn a little to the right and you can see mountains 125 miles away. "The fence" stretches across his front yard, a thousand feet high. Train Rock, Eagle Rock Mesa, Brigham's Tomb, the Big Leader, the Big Indian, and Castle Butte. They look only a stone's throw away, and yet they are eight miles distant. In that high altitude, distances are deceiving, but the beauty is not. It's always there.

The Big Rock Door Mesa had been given that name by the Navajos because of a narrow defile that went south between Tsay-Kizzi Mesa and Old Baldy Mesa, into the Navajo Reservation just two miles away. A trail through the canyon provided the Indians with convenient entrance and exit. As a result, Harry's location, at the northern ertance to the Big Rock Door, provided an excellent site for a trading post, which gave him added reason for choosing it.

Even as John Wetherill had done a number of years before, near the Moonlight Waters, Harry Goulding set up a makeshift counter in front

Harry Goulding standing atop Double Arch
PHOTOGRAPHER UNKNOWN

Afternoon shadows in Monument Valley
PHOTOGRAPH BY ROBERT Z. BRUCKMAN

of his tents and prepared to trade. And the Indian reaction, though it took longer, was exactly the same as it had been at Oljeto. For the first years, while he traded from his tents, the Indians kept their silence and traded with the white man. But when it began to look as if he intended to stay, they asked him to leave.

It all came to a head on a day Harry will long remember. An unusual number of Indians were trading, and then, abruptly, they stopped and gathered about the tents that held the trading supplies. There was nothing in the way of preamble. One of the Navajos asked Harry how long he planned to stay in their valley. Goulding pointed to his tent and answered, "When my hair is the color of that, I may leave. But not before." The Indians grew sullen, and, as Harry would tell you, "the atmosphere sure got thick." He was scared but he couldn't let them know that.

He stuck out their bluff and held his ground. In time, the crisis passed. Someone laughed and cracked a joke. Harry laughed back. Trading started again, and the Indians returned to their homes. There was never any trouble from that moment on. The Indians accepted Harry as a friend and he never failed them. Their antagonism probably had been in the nature of a test. The way it turned out was most acceptable to them, and they approved of the tall, friendly white man.

Harry ran sheep in the valley, as he had back in Colorado and New Mexico, for almost ten years. He enlarged his flock, buying every animal from the Indians. His flock soon became one of the largest in the valley, and the Indians, with their wonderful ability to name people and places aptly, called Harry "T'pay-eh-nez," the "Long man with the sheep." It was a name that sticks by him even today, though the sheep and Harry have long since parted company.

That initial year in the place of the monuments also drew another first. Two artists came from Oklahoma City and signed the guest register as the very first in a long line of geologists, archaeologists, anthropologists, painters, writers, well drillers, mining men, movie makers, and just plain tourists. With two tents serving as home and place of business there was no guest room for visitors. But the Gouldings have a neat habit of never turning anyone away, a custom which was born right then. They offered to share their own tent and the artists stayed in the valley of the monuments for fourteen days, drinking in the magic of the enchanted valley and trying to capture in oils the undercurrent of romance that is always there.

The Gouldings lived in their twelve-by-fourteen-foot tent for almost four years. At the end of eleven months of self-imposed isolation they went north to find if city lights held anything for them. They did not. After eight days away from their beloved Monument Valley, Mike wanted to go back "home," and back they went.

In 1927, they began to build a real home to take the place of the tents. Two trappers, on their way through from Houserock Valley and the Kaibab Forest, were invited to stay in the valley to trap and help with the building. They accepted the invitation and stayed with the Gouldings for the better part of a year. The trading post was finished in 1928. It was a solid two-story affair, with the store and all the supplies on the first floor and living quarters above. All the visitors who came to Monument Valley during the next years, stayed there in the castle of the King and Queen of Monument Valley. A one-room stone cabin was constructed the same year and provided extra space for guests. A second cottage was erected several years later, and the post was composed of only these three buildings until the movies came, in 1938. In the years that followed, an additional room was added to the back of the trading post, a dining room and kitchen was built, and several CCC bunk houses were brought in from nearby Kanab and reassembled in the valley.

Harry had his turn at the Mitchell-Merrick legend soon after he came to the valley of the monuments. He was befriended by the last survivor of the twelve tribesmen who had buried the silver mine behind tons of rock and sand. The old Indian told Harry many things about the valley, often hinting about his knowledge as to the secret location of the Navajo silver, though never openly discussing it. But Goulding had heard the legend many times, and quickly put two and two together.

In later years, Harry remembered the old man and sent for him. When he came they talked of many things, and, at length, Harry asked him about the mine. "Your people are poor," Harry said. "Reopen the mine. Take out some silver for yourself. It does no one any good where it is now. Help your people with the money it would bring to you."

Goulding offered to provide saddles for the old man's burros, plus all the other necessary equipment to transport the ore from the mine to the trading post. He offered to see also that the crude ore reached the railroad, and the profits would be shared among them. At length the old man was convinced. Yes, here was the way to get the cattle and sheep The People needed so badly. Perhaps it was the thing to do.

So one day he appeared at the Monument Valley trading post, leading his string of burros. True to his word, Harry completely outfitted the expedition and watched it go its way. The Indian had little to say, but when preparations were completed, he plodded off to the northwest, toward San Juan River and the distant Mossbacks. He headed directly into the roughest of terrain, land cut by numerous washes and barrancas, probably intending to lose anyone who had even the slightest intention of following him.

Shortly after he had disappeared, rain came to the valley. Rain in Monument Valley almost invariably comes in one way—a hard pelting downfall of short duration. But here was the exception. Rain came this time as a penetrating and miserable drizzle. It chilled to the bone, continuing all that day, and into the next. And even on the third day it lingered on in the same way, overcast and sodden.

Toward the end of the third day the Indian reappeared in Harry's camp. He was alone, and on foot. And he was scared, so badly scared that he could scarcely talk to Harry. But at length the white man figured out what had happened. The old Navajo had rheumatism. Probably by the end of the very first day, as the caravan was wending its way around the wet arroyos, the rain and dampness began to settle within his bones. By the end of the second day, he felt much worse, and the convictions he had supported only vaguely at the beginning of the trip were now beginning to assume fantastic shapes. Surely the gods were angry with this wretched old man. For helping to contrive the plan to reopen the mine, his gods had been aroused and were both actually and literally showering pain and misfortune upon him. When the third day dawned in the same wet way, he knew for sure that he was going against the will of his deities. He threw all plans aside, abandoned camp, and made great haste in getting back to the trading post.

Harry's attempt to locate the mine proved to be a failure like the others, though his held a somewhat humorous ending. Because he had persuaded the Indian to try to reopen the mine, he had brought about disapproval of the gods, and he had caused the onset of the painful rheumatism. To correct the evil, and pacify the gods, Harry must pay for a "sing," when a sand painting would be drawn and the wisest and best medicine men of the tribe would be called upon to prove their healing abilities.

For that "sing" the old man required something very significant. He requested that he be taken to a piñon tree at the base of Merrick Butte. There he secured a branch and a piece of the root. These things later were reduced to charcoal and the old man was covered from head to foot with the black powder. The reasons were obvious. Doubtless the old tribal leader had been present at the Mitchell-Merrick episode of so many years before. As a young warrior, he probably had taken part in the killing of Merrick and perhaps Mitchell as well. Now, apparently, he believed his sins were cumulative and had resulted in his present illness. By covering himself with the charcoal of the piñon he was somehow—in the mystic way of the Indian—cleansing himself of the evil in these past deeds and no longer need feel fear of retribution.

The sand painting was drawn, the Navajo placed upon it, and the ceremony begun. Strangely enough, the Indian completely recovered and lived to a ripe old age. It all cost Harry Goulding one hundred dollars, but actually, he had not wasted his money. He had learned a valuable lesson. Let someone else search for the mine. He was through with it.

In the many years Harry has lived in the valley there have been not a few others who have thought they were the chosen ones, the ones who would certainly find the legendary silver. Even today, they appear in Monument Valley, mysterious and close in their actions. Invariably, they do not stop to talk, but disappear into the back country in their automobiles. Then, within a matter of a few days, they are back at the trading post, most of them coming in on foot, hot and thirsty and complaining to the heavens about their bad luck. While Harry is helping to free their car, which is either stuck, or, most likely, broken down, and while waiting for a new part to come from Kayenta, or perhaps Cameron, the truth comes out. And the truth is always the same story. The disappointed silver-seeker has a map, a very secret map, passed down to him by someone who had actually visited the Navajo silver mine, but just simply didn't have time to go back and find it again. Just as invariably, the map is always wrong. Rarely is it even similar to the actual country.

Though far from Wall Street and its economic crises, Monument Valley suffered with the rest of the nation during the depression. There were only a few visitors. Mutton was not bringing a price high enough to warrant taking the sheep to market. There was only one thing to do with the wool and that was to make saddle blankets and rugs. But while these items piled up in trading-post stock rooms, the price succeeded in reaching rock bottom. Beautiful creations, painstakingly woven by the patient Indian women, brought only $1.25 or less. Even into the early thirties the situation did not improve. There was no money in the valley, and very little food for anyone to eat. Harry tells of making a can of Karo syrup last an entire winter, though serving as dessert at every meal. Often a piece of bread was rubbed about the rim of the can, and the imagination was called upon to do the rest.

People of less spirit and determination than Harry and Mike Goulding would never have weathered out the lean and hard years of the depression. But their irrepressible love for the land made them cling to it through every setback and each apparent sign of defeat. Then at last their love and persistence paid off as the movies came into the valley. But that's a story in itself.

Today, partially due to the movies, the Monument Valley Trading Post and Lodge has all the appearance and aspects of a small town. With the years have come such conveniences as electricity, refrigeration, deep freeze, and hot and cold running water.

When Goulding first began to call Monument Valley home, the Navajos were using it as a part of their grazing land. The Piutes had all gone north to their newly accepted greener pastures, leaving Monument Valley and the San Juan country open to Navajo sheep and goats. As the summer came, so did the Navajos and their flocks. In the north, white sheepmen also espied the southern grazing lands. And inevitably, conflict developed as it always has between white and red man. For the whites it usually was another victory. They always seemed to have the advantage of larger flocks and greater man power.

As a resident witness to the conflict that was spreading about him yearly, Harry Goulding made efforts to bring the then-existent boundary of the reservation north to the San Juan River. He became a personal friend of the government agent at Tuba City, applied the famous Goulding persistence, and finally succeeded in doing what he had set out to do. The proposal was offered Congress, passed both houses, and was signed into law by President Hoover as his last official act of office on March 1, 1933. So on that date, Harry became the only white man to own land within the vast Navajo

View looking east from Hoskinnini Mesa

PHOTOGRAPH BY GIBBS M. SMITH

Indian Reservation. There are many traders in Indian territory, but their lands are leased from the government for a period of years. In eleven years of public domain, Harry was the only person to avail himself of the opportunity to own some of that precious land. It cost him $320; today I'm sure he would refuse $100,000.

His years of Monument Valley residence have endeared him to the hearts of the Indians who live there. They know Harry as a friend, because they know and appreciate what he has done for them. He has become a trusted white man who shares their confidences. And to watch Harry with his Indians, you can easily see how he has won his way into their hearts. A Navajo's wealth usually is measured by the amount of silver he owns. But when he needs money for supplies he occasionally has to pawn some of his precious silver. Necklaces, bracelets, rings, and earrings, bow guards, concho belts, and decorated buttons are all likely to end up in the white man's trading post, pawned for credit. The legal pawn limit set by the Indian Service is six months to a year. After that it may be sold by the trader. But Harry doesn't sell pawn that way. In July of 1950 I saw him finally release a bracelet pawned in 1942 and never redeemed. Though the rafters in Harry's store are covered with pawn, only rarely is any of it sold. And that's only one reason why the Indians accept Harry Goulding as a close and personal friend. There are many others.

In past years, Harry has celebrated the Christmas season by helping with a gigantic Christmas party. The parties are planned by Hugh D. Smith, referred to as "Shine" Smith by everyone who knows him, who is an ordained Presbyterian minister and has spent the years since World War I spreading his religion in Monument Valley. Shine Smith's Christmas parties have become phenomenal. For months in advance, the people of the valley area look forward to it. Carloads of candy and clothing make it a gala affair for the Indian. If you would ask Harry why he shares expenses every year for that Christmas party, he would tell you about happy Indians on our happiest of holidays. Harry gets paid back for his goodness in the way that is most rewarding of all.

Perhaps a thousand visitors a year come to the valley, and the number is steadily increasing, for anyone who once sees it goes forth as a disciple to proclaim its fabulous wonder and beauty. It inspires all people. It makes artists paint and writers compose with a new fire and energy. Monument Valley is just that way.

The second World War brought something new to the place of the monuments, and again it was Harry Goulding who helped to bring it there. When certain metals were badly needed for the war effort, Harry went prospecting. He never had amounted to much as a prospector, but probably that was only because he had never really tried. And then, too, there was the Mitchell-Merrick episode which always quickly discouraged any ideas he may have had of being a hot-shot prospector.

Navajo home life. With mano and metate, this Navajo woman grinds her corn as did her ancestors for generations past.

PHOTOGRAPHER UNKNOWN

Atop one of the buttes, he found a group of surface boulders that bore traces of yellow stain. It was the very thing that Harry had been searching for. On returning to the lodge he called the officials of the Vanadium Corporation of America. Inspection by government officials followed. It satisfied them, too. Soon Navajo work teams were picking at the yellow-stained rock and loading it into heavy trucks. A new mineral boom resulted, and it hasn't ended yet. For the yellow stuff was uranium ore. In the Shinarump conglomerate that caps so many of the buttes and mesas they found the material vastly important to the Age of the Atom. The heavy trucks still groan out of the valley, chewing up the sand roads and carrying tons of the yellowish-green ore up through Mexican Hat and Blanding to the far-distant railroad.

With or without paved roads, the number of tourists that go into Monument Valley will increase as the years go by. Across from Tsay-Kizzi Mesa, on the other side of the Big Rock Door, is Old Baldy Mesa. Harry laughs when he tells you about that. It's on his land—a part of his 640 acres— and he can't even reach the top without a parachute. But when the tourists begin to come in greater numbers and Harry loses his personal contact with the visitors, I think he's likely to make a retreat. And he'll probably find a way to get up on Old Baldy to be alone with his valley.

SCIENCE AND THE DREAMER

During the middle years of the depression there were other events of importance that took their turn at occupying the stage in Monument Valley. There was Everett Ruess, the youthful romantic, and there was the government-sponsored expeditions into the valley area during the years of 1933, 1934, and 1935.

The government ventures, with their great scope and high ambitions, were something relatively new to the valley itself. Actually, it is true, men of science had already been peering into the valley for a number of years. But only rarely did they have the time, money, and backing to linger there long enough to dispel any of the clouds of the unknown that clung to the area. The few scientific studies made there had been reconnaissance and nothing more. The Geological and Geographical Survey of the Territories, under Dr. F. V. Hayden, between 1873 and 1878, surveyed areas in Colorado, Idaho, New Mexico, Utah, and Wyoming, comprising about 100,000 square miles. However, this extensive survey did not include lands far enough west to contain Monument Valley. The United States Geological Survey of 1884 gave particular emphasis to San Juan County, in Utah, and Coconino County, in Arizona, but had little to do with the place of the monuments.

Dr. Herbert E. Gregory, noted authority on geology and geography of the Southwest, visited the enchanted valley a number of times to inspect the curious geological formations that are so manifest there. In the years from 1908 to 1910 he succeeded in mapping the complete Navajo Indian Reservation as it existed at that time, and, in succeeding years, he published several papers of especial regional interest. Arthur A. Baker investigated the area, under the auspices of the U. S. Geological Survey in the summer of 1928, and offered his highly informative bulletin on the geology of the Monument Valley-Navajo Mountain region in 1936. Interesting and informative as all these papers and studies came to be from the standpoint of the geologist, they only barely touched upon the natural phenomena and archaeological sites of the valley.

Because of the need for authentic and unbiased information on topog-

The Mittens

PHOTOGRAPH BY RONALD W. HARRIS

raphy and the scenic features, geology, archaeology, ethnology, and plant and animal life of the area, the idea for the Monument Valley-Rainbow Bridge expeditions germinated and grew. Ansel Franklin Hall, who had directed numerous other expeditions into various parts of the Southwest in preceding years, fostered the idea and drew together others who had similar interests. General plans were created and submitted for initial approval, through the office of the Director of the National Park Service, to the Commissioner of Indian Affairs, the Commissioner of the General Land Office, the Director of the United States Geological Survey, and the consulting archaeologist for the Department of the Interior. Approval was granted immediately by each department, and application was next made to the Secretary of the Interior for an expedition to carry out the intended scientific field studies on the federal lands administered by the various bureaus. Again, permission was granted.

For such an ambitious venture, Mr. Hall, who was designated general director of the expedition, found it necessary to form a responsible and talented party. To this end a sizeable crew was recruited from the teaching staffs and advanced students of the University of California, Stanford University, the University of Minnesota, Princeton University, the University of Illinois, New York University, Pratt Institute, Carnegie Institute of Technology, the Museum of Northern Arizona, and other institutions. With the selection of party and assemblage of supplies, the adventure was about to begin.

Assistance was offered promptly from many quarters. The Bureau of Indian Affairs provided a storeroom for instruments and supplies at Kayenta, the settlement that was used also as the major base for the expedition operations. John Wetherill, then custodian of the Navajo National Monument, assembled animals for the various pack trains and allowed his ranch at Kayenta to be used as a center of activities. The U. S. Forest Service assisted in matters relating to the clearance and shipment of supplies from the railroad base, 190 miles away, at Flagstaff. The U. S. Army Engineers Corps supplied plane tables, transits, alidades, barometers, and other instruments necessary for the proper mapping of the area to be explored. The U. S. Army Air Corps furnished an aerial camera with which later were secured photographs used in furnishing details for a topographic map of the area. The Museum of Northern Arizona, that noteworthy institution of scientific learning near Flagstaff, also supplied much in the way of scientific supplies and instruments that were necessary for the planned archaeological reconnaissance.

The 1933 expedition probably was the most ambitious of the three successive undertakings, and consumed the greater portion of three months—June 3 through August 21. As was expected, it was found to be impossible to explore thoroughly an area of more than three thousand square miles.

An airplane, station wagons and trucks, burros and horses, even boats for the San Juan, were used in covering the various parts of the area. Activity that first summer was confined to several wide strips across the region that contained abundant features of scientific interest. In the two summers that followed, the same areas were covered in a more thorough manner and a few new regions were explored. Nevertheless, even after three summers of exploration, large portions did, and still do, remain untouched.

Those expeditions, of the depression years, proved to be of great value. But in many respects they asked more questions, and only partially satisfactory answers were obtained. However, one thing was certain then, as it remains true today. Monument Valley, and the surrounding area, provides one of the last remaining areas in the United States in need of intense exploration and scientific study that is not a matter of months, but one of years.

Also in the heart of those lean years, remote and far-distant from the cold and calculating eye of scientific investigation, came the young romantic, Everett Ruess.

In a country that seems to be dreamlike in itself it is only natural and right that there should be dreamers. And it is only right that in a land as romantic as Monument Valley there should be a story like that of Everett Ruess. From the very beginning, when the great Negro, Estéban, came into the land with his lusts and desires for a freedom he had never known, there have been many dreamers in the land that contains Monument Valley. Many had dreams that were like those of Estéban—shallow dreams of wealth and fortune. But the romantic dreams that seem to be our own secret wishes come true were made to live by Everett Ruess. As a young man of eighteen he had a dream in which he saw himself, as a great adventurer, fighting through green jungles, pulling himself up the faces of sheer cliffs, and wandering through lands of romance as no man had ever done. Though his dreams were always unattainable, he made them that way, kept searching for them, and always found great satisfaction. He died when we who know no better would say he should just have begun to live, but he had already found more in his few years than the average person finds in all his three score and ten. Everett Ruess is the romanticist we all would be if we had the courage and fortitude to really live our lives as he did his.

No man forgets his dreams, though often they become far distant and faded, but Everett Ruess had no chance to forget. He lived his. He loved to write and to paint, so he went to that country where those things come naturally. He was not a good writer, and certainly not an exceptional painter, but he knew it. And despite that, he went ahead so that he could learn. At eighteen he started travelling by horse and burro and by foot through the lands of southern Utah and northern Arizona. That was in 1931. He was twenty when his travels ended. That was in 1934. During those years between 1931 and 1934 he went often into Monument Valley. Harry Goulding remembers him well. Ruess made his headquarters there in the shadow of the Big Rock Door Mesa with T'pay-eh-nez. He became

Hardy high desert plants cover the floor of Monument Valley
PHOTOGRAPH BY GIBBS M. SMITH

intimate with a large portion of the country that most people never see or even hear about. He lived among the ranchers and the Indians, danced the antelope dance with the Hopi people, learned the difficult Navajo language, made friends with every trader in the territory, and was a familiar figure over all that land.

It is easy to see why he came back again and again to Monument Valley. This was the very stuff that his dreams made made of. He was living a dream by being there and writing and painting of the monuments.

On November 11, 1934, Ruess left Escalante, Utah, on a trip into one of the wildest and most desolate regions of all North America. Into the fantastically wonderful country about the mouths of the Escalante and San Juan rivers he ventured alone. That fall and winter Everett Ruess did not go into Monument Valley, nor did he ever go there again.

After he had been absent on his journey for two months, his parents began casual questions, still not too seriously worried, for they had grown used to the long two- or three-month disappearances of their son. When their inquiries turned up no information, they became vaguely disturbed. The young man was not declared officially missing until February 14, 1935, more than three months after he had last been seen. There followed a very extensive search which covered much of the area into which he had disappeared. Miners, herders, Indians, traders, all joined in the hunt. But there was no sign of the young dreamer. Finally, in a cave near Davis Canyon on the Colorado they found his half-starved burros and the remains of what was most likely his last campfire. But nothing else. His pack, his personal belongings, everything had disappeared with him. Hundreds of miles of canyons and mesa tops were combed for some further trace of him, but still no sign. There could be only one conclusion and that was even more mysterious. Ruess evidently had been murdered, presumably for his valuable pack equipment. His body must have been buried or hidden somewhere in that trackless country.

But who would kill him, and why? He was a personal friend of everyone who lived in that country. There are many more questions than answers in the strange story of Everett Ruess. It rests there today. No trace of him has ever been found, although those other semi-romanticists, who live their dreams by preserving the deeds of their heroes, claim that Everett Ruess, with his writing pad and paint brush, still haunts the canyons of the Monument Valley country, living his dreams. Perhaps he does, for now Everett Ruess has become immortal.

HOLLYWOOD INVASION

Many people who have never known Monument Valley by name have known that it existed somewhere in our land because they saw its splendid spires and buttes in several of the Hollywood movies that have been made there since the film capital first included it in its location repertory, in 1938. The account of how the movie-makers "discovered" Monument Valley and first went there is as colorful as any tale could be.

In that year of 1938, after pulling out of the depression and struggling through the middle thirties, Harry Goulding and his Navajos both were at economic low ebb. The absence of visitors in any number and the low prices paid for Indian products meant that both white man and red man had suffered. It was early in that year that Harry heard, through friends in Hollywood, that a Western movie was about to be made. At that time a Western movie to be made on location, as this one would be, was somewhat of a rarity. And it offered Harry an opportunity he had long been waiting for. His land deserved recognition and could prove a valuable asset to any movie. In the long run it would provide needed money for the Indians and it would also attract more visitors to this land of the monuments. All he needed to do was to convince the movie people of his own certainty that Monument Valley was the ideal place to film a Western production.

Harry reacted in his usual manner. With Mike beside him he set off for California with every cent they possessed—sixty dollars, and all the confidence in the world. It was truly a memorable journey. They practiced strict budgeting from the first, eating fewer meals, and carefully watching hotel bills. They arrived in Hollywood, and the first thing they received was free advice. "Turn right around and go back to your valley," another friend told him. "Unless you know someone on the *inside* of one of those studios, you don't stand a chance of even getting in, let alone talking with someone important." A person with less stamina than Harry would have ordered a retreat right then, but Harry had a reason for not giving up. He had Monument Valley, and a great love for his land.

Shrugging off the warning, and warming to the task ahead, Harry left Mike behind while he headed for United Artists studios. He was armed with the only ammunition he had brought along. A large stack of photographs of his beloved valley. Loaded with these pictures and trying to appear confident he sauntered casually into the reception room of one of the studio administration buildings facing the street. Spotting the receptionist behind a glass window he explained to her just exactly what he had come for. A Western movie was to be filmed, and he knew just the place to film it. She smiled sweetly and asked if he had an appointment.

"No."

Did he know anyone in the studio?

"No."

She shook her head. "Sorry. You have to know someone."

Once again, Harry wouldn't say die. He insisted that he should see someone, and she insisted that he couldn't. But he wore her down. At length she gave in and placed a call. To the man on the other end of the line she offered a hasty summary of what this man from the reservation wanted. Then she listened to stern warnings to get him out of there right away.

The girl hung up the receiver and smiled sadly at Harry, who had overheard all the conversation. He was a bit taken aback, but quickly recovered. "Well," he said, "back on the reservation we always have lots of time, and we're never too busy to see anyone who drops in to talk with us. So, if you don't mind, I'll just make myself at home and wait. I brought along my bed roll just in case."

"You can't stay," she said.

"Don't know why not," he answered, and made himself comfortable in a large arm chair.

With that, the phone was busy again as the receptionist called the same number a second time. She explained once more to the man who answered.

"He can't do that," the voice ordered.

"He can and is." She said this as she eyed Harry, resting comfortably in the plush chair as if he intended to stay awhile.

"Well, I'll show *him* who's boss around here! . . ." and the receiver clicked.

Harry heard footsteps coming down the hallway, and wondered for a moment if perhaps he had gone too far. But before all confidence had left him the door into the reception room opened and a short man bristled out. He looked up at Harry and stopped all forward motion. On both sides there was a brief moment of indecision and surprise. In that moment Harry did the wisest thing he could possibly have done. He turned toward the man so that the top picture under his left arm was in plain view. The short man looked down and his eye caught the picture. Quickly Harry turned and displayed the picture on the top of the bundle under the other arm. The man's interest increased. He looked for a moment longer, then smiled in a friendly way.

"What are those pictures of?" he asked.

Harry explained.

"I can spare a few minutes to talk with you about your Monument Valley," the movie-maker said.

The short man proved to be location director for the new Western movie, and that "few minutes" developed into hours. Could a movie be made there in the valley? What kind of facilities were at hand? Was it truly as remarkable and beautiful as the pictures showed it to be? And many other questions. At length the man brought in another man, a director by the name of John Ford, and together they examined the pictures carefully, one after the other, spreading them all over the room, and all the time asking more and more questions. Hours passed.

Then the two men called in Walter Wanger, producing chief at United Artists, to talk with Harry. When Wanger came, there were more questions, more discussions, more examinations of all the pictures. Then, some eight hours after Harry had come into the office, came the big, important question. Could you handle one hundred people in three days to begin shooting of a Western movie?

Harry was taken aback. Three days? Why so soon? The monuments had been there for quite a spell and would certainly stay there longer than another three days. How about a week or two?

But Harry had things to learn about Hollywood. "The first thing you have to learn," said Walter Wanger, "is that when Hollywood wants to do something right now, they *do* it right now. Can you be ready in three days?"

"Well," said Harry, "I suppose so, but it's going to cost a whale of a lot of money."

"Lesson number two," said Wanger. "Money is no object. Can we do it or not?"

"Yes, I guess we probably can."

Then things began to happen. A check was made out and handed to Harry, and he was hustled off to return to his valley to prepare for an invasion. He told Mike the wonderful news, and that very night they headed for Flagstaff.

In Flagstaff they stopped at Babbitt Brothers General Store to order the necessary supplies for the hundred people who soon would be on hand. But once again Harry had underestimated the power of Hollywood. Eleven trucks, being loaded with merchandise, stood parked in front of the store. As Harry stared at them, Ed Babbitt came running excitedly out of the store. Breathlessly, he explained. Harry Goulding was already far behind times. A group of men already had flown in from Hollywood and ordered all the things that were to be needed in the valley. Everything from canned carrots to tar paper was loaded up, waiting only for Harry to make a final check and send it on its way.

Yes, Hollywood, Harry Goulding soon found out, does things in a big way. He examined the eleven truck loads of supplies and found great quantities of all the things they would need, plus many other "luxury" items he would never have thought to include. Another day passed and then the movies began coming to Monument Valley in full force. John Ford, John Wayne, Thomas Mitchell, Claire Trevor, Andy Devine, and almost a hundred others, stars, technicians, and skilled workmen, came in to film their movie against the majestic backdrop of Monument Valley. The resulting picture, released in late 1938 was the Academy Award winner "Stagecoach."

Movie-goers who are familiar with the valley were amused by the fact that the stagecoach was first shown to be going in one direction and then the other. At the beginning of the movie the journey commences in the shadow of the Mittens. Some reels and many adventures later, the trip ends in the very same spot. Perhaps the travellers had round-trip tickets.

In addition to being the culmination of an unforgettable adventure "Stagecoach" achieved the very ends that Harry Goulding had been working for. Thousands of dollars were paid in salaries to the Indians who worked as laborers and movie extras. Everyone, from Hoskinnini-begay to the poorest member of the tribe, had the opportunity to work, and they eagerly seized the chance. The Monument Valley trading post was the main target every evening as Navajos lined up to redeem their pawn, and to buy blankets, food, and supplies that they needed for the winter ahead. "Stagecoach" won an Academy Award with the Indians, too. It helped them at a time when they needed help in a big way.

But the help was only temporary, and it wasn't long before Harry was back once again in Hollywood to encourage movie production among the monuments. Friends in strategic places did and still do tip him off when a Western adventure is about to be filmed on location. But, often, Harry waited for no such prodding. In past years he made trips to Hollywood almost yearly just to lure Hollywood into Monument Valley.

In 1940, Harry learned that United Artists was preparing another Western thriller, a picture that would recount the feats of Kit Carson. And this time it was Edward Small who heard from Harry Goulding. But the second attempt was much easier than the first had been. "Oh, yes," said Small when Harry called him, "you're the long-legged trader from the Indian reservation." Harry got in to see Edward Small on that introduction, and he succeeded in getting another movie crew to come into his valley. It was "Kit Carson," starring Jon Hall. In a way it was almost ironic that seventy-seven years after Kit Carson had pursued Hoskinnini and his people into the place of the monuments, descendants of those same Indians were assisting in the filming of a movie lauding the feats of the Indian scout. Time indeed plays strange tricks.

Metro-Goldwyn-Mayer discovered the valley in 1941, when the location crew of "Billy the Kid" came in and filmed large portions of that picture, for the first time showing Monument Valley in technicolor.

The movies returned in force in 1944, but this time it was only a second company which filmed background shots, then returned to Hollywood to put them behind a production. What came out was "The Harvey Girls,"

Movie camp for THE SEARCHERS, corner of Hollywood and Vine. There were no accommodations nearer than Flagstaff for the sizeable crew, so everyone stayed here, except for the stars who were up at the Lodge

PHOTOGRAPH BY RICHARD E. KLINCK

starring Judy Garland. Harry Goulding will never forget that one. In the movie, Monument Valley can be seen out of the windows of the train that provides most of the movie's setting. Hollywood magic again! Though Monument Valley is farthest from a railroad of any place in the entire United States, the Atchison, Topeka, and Santa Fe was shown to be running directly between the Mittens.

"My Darling Clementine" was the next big production brought into the valley and resulted in the construction of the first permanent set. At a cost of $250,000 "The town too tough to die," Tombstone, Arizona, was recreated in Monument Valley. It had the same Bird Cage Theatre, the same Mansion House Hotel, and the same bars. But despite the similarity, Tombstone itself could never claim the prime distinguishing feature between the Hollywood imitation and the real thing—the great red monuments of Monument Valley.

When the movie was finished and the last Navajo had received his pay check, the entire movie set was turned over to the tribal council to be rented to other studios that came into the valley or disposed of in a manner the Indians saw fit. For five years it rested quietly in the sun, disconcerting to visitors who were discovering Monument Valley for the first time. Blinking in amazement they would hurriedly survey their road maps to find the name of this tiny village huddled in the middle of the majestic loneliness. In 1951, the make-believe Tombstone was sold for salvage, dismantled, and carted away, removing an unsightly and unnatural blemish from the sun-caressed valley of the monuments.

John Ford returned to the valley for a third time, in 1947, to film the exterior shots of "Fort Apache." The fort itself was built in Hollywood and all connected shots were filmed against prop backgrounds which resulted in some incongruities when the movie was tied together with the real scenery.

In 1948, came "She Wore a Yellow Ribbon," a movie that sang the praises of the United States Cavalry, in technicolor. More of the haunting magnificence of the valley was recorded than had ever before been put on film. The red rocks, white clouds, and royal blue skies performed admirably before the cameras. One hundred stars and technicians were housed at the Goulding post for that movie. A supplementary camp was set up nearby to house an additional five hundred people. Rather than build complete new sets it was decided that the actual buildings of Harry's lodge and trading post would be used. Certain additions and improvements were made; and before the first camera started turning, the Monument Valley Trading Post and Lodge had been turned into a cavalry post of the late 1860's.

Again it was only exterior shots that were filmed in the valley, but by far the greatest portion of the picture takes place out-of-doors. The few interior shots were spliced in after the company returned to Hollywood. And no wonder that they were filmed in Hollywood. The inside of the movie's trading post and tavern was Harry Goulding's dining room. The cavalry company headquarters was actually filled with flour, salt, and canned goods, for it was the real trading post. And John Wayne's personal billet, from which, according to the movie, he came proudly charging every morning, was really the potato cellar.

River scenes were shot just east of Bluff, on the San Juan, but one of the most remarkable shots concerns the buffalo shown in the film. Actually, the buffalo were a part of the largest remaining herd in the United States, located far to the west of Monument Valley in Houserock Valley. But— and it's a pleasure to hear Harry Goulding tell this—he sat there on the porch of his lodge and watched a group of cavalrymen ride to the top of a tiny knoll and point to the west—at nothing. "Sure enough," says Harry, "When the movie came out, there was Johnnie Agar pointing at the buffalo

A scene from the film *Stagecoach* starring John Wayne
PHOTOGRAPHER UNKNOWN

way over in Houserock Valley, and they saw them!" Once again, recurring Hollywood magic.

Harry told me of a few of the many wild stagecoach rides and horseback rides he has seen take place across the rough land out in front of his trading post. Only Hollywood would do it, he said. No one else would be crazy enough.

Numerous other film companies have made the trek into Monument Valley, too. In fact, almost every major studio has been there at least once. But, except for the ones mentioned above, these others all have been second units which filmed only a few background shots and took them back to Hollywood. Even the movie capital cannot match the wondrous beauty of the monuments. The favorite season is September, October, and November, when photography is at its best.

But our fast-moving civilization has temporarily demanded too much of the valley. In order that Hollywood may enjoy the speed it has become used to, it has taken up the practice of flying stars, technicians, and portions of the necessary equipment in by air to the location where the movie will be filmed. Heavy equipment still must come by road, but a sizeable portion can be flown in. And that means a large airstrip is needed close to the point of production, one that is larger than the one available at the present time in Monument Valley. And true to style, Harry is working toward this end.

First, he approached the governor of Utah and asked for an appropriation so that a larger airstrip could be financed. Next, though the land was in the state of Utah, it was also a part of the Indian lands, and to obtain it Harry would have to trade a small piece of his land for another piece for the airstrip. No such thing had ever been done before and it required a special act of Congress to make it legal. But Harry won out, and now he has that exchange of land. Even so, developments went backward as well as forward. While trying to secure the land exchange, a new Utah governor entered the statehouse and all fund appropriations were revoked.

Before leaving the subject of movies in Monument Valley there is a most unusual sidelight that has proved to be very interesting over a period of years and has assumed somewhat the status of a legend among the movie people. When John Ford first came into the valley with his "Stagecoach" company, he was doubtful as to the reliability of the weather, something very vital in film production. That doubt paved the way for his introduction to Hosteen Tso—Mister Big, or Fatso, as he became generally known.

Hosteen Tso is a Navajo medicine man of great renown among his people, and also somewhat of a joker, as Harry Goulding has found out through experience. Recently Fatso was low on necessary cash, and looked around for something to pawn. He owned a large four-wheeled wagon, and settled on that as a likely choice. Shortly after pawning it at one post and spending the pawn money, he returned there with a sad tale of his plight. Seems the family had no wood, and he had no way of gettting any more for them since his wagon was in hock. The trader, sympathizing to an extent he later discovered was too great, lent the wagon to the big man for just long enough to get the necessary wood.

With the wagon once more in his possession, Fatso promptly went to another trading post and pawned it again, later returning with the same story he had used before. It succeeded just as well the second time, and it was not until he had successfully pawned the wagon three times that the traders became wise and closed in on him. When caught with the wagon, he blithely confessed his trick and smiled with a sense of supreme achievement.

But Fatso's prowess as a medicine man was even greater than his abilities as a pawning artist. And, with him in mind, Harry promised John Ford fabulous things about the weather in the never-never land of the monuments.

"Just have your weather orders in by four o'clock a day in advance and I'll have Old Fatso fix you up," Harry facetiously told the movie director. And that's just how it happened. If a clear blue sky was wanted, with perhaps just a few snowball clouds in it, Fatso would see to it that that was exactly what they received. But then, that was easy. How about something complicated? How about a thunder storm, or a dust storm? Those should have been a lot harder—but Fatso brought them around too.

One day, during the filming of "Stagecoach," Ford remarked that he had a bit of an unusual order for the following day. He wanted clear blue skies for a few shots in the morning, and a dust storm in the afternoon. Harry didn't say anything. He just passed the word on to Hosteen Tso. The following day dawned bright and clear, with just the right amount of thin, wispy clouds. Shooting went ahead on schedule, but dragged out a bit along toward noon. "Better hurry up," Harry advised Ford. "Don't forget you have a dust storm coming up for this afternoon." Ford looked at him doubtfully. A dust storm? It never looked any less like a dust storm. But, already respecting the combination of Harry and Fatso, he hastened completion of the morning's shooting.

And, sure enough, right on schedule, the dust storm arrived. It materialized from out of nowhere quite suddenly. Luckily, cameras were set for action and all the props were on hand. The takes were completed as rapidly as possible, and just in time. The dusty prelude was followed by a full-

Erosion has created the massive formations of Monument Valley

PHOTOGRAPH BY ROBERT Z. BRUCKMAN

fledged storm that stopped everything with its swirling sand and heavy winds. Hosteen Tso retained a firm grip on the elements.

Right then, John Ford stopped laughing at Fatso and gave him an honored place on his list of essential personnel. Now, whenever Ford goes out on location to the valley of the monuments or a nearby area, such as during the filming of "Wagonmaster" and "Rio Grande" at close-by Moab, Utah, Fatso is the person placed at the very top of the payroll roster. Maybe it's being superstitious, but why take chances?

Remember the thunderstorm in "She Wore a Yellow Ribbon"? That, too, was a special order. Thunderstorms are fairly rare and are unusually evasive when there is particular need for one. But there was a command performance in "Yellow Ribbon." Three hundred people watched in the shadow of the South Mitten as Hosteen Tso called on his rain gods to send forth a storm. And three hundred people got wet when it came.

John Ford was awed by Monument Valley, and he was awed by the performances given by old Hosteen Tso. In the guest book at the Monument Valley Trading Post after the filming of "Fort Apache" he wrote, "Again I am sorry to say *'Adios'* to you and your hospitality. My thanks also to old Fatso who gave us such wonderful weather."

It all sounds strange in our day. "Impossible," you might say. Navajo medicine contains many of the dark and mystic elements our world knew many centuries ago. As such it is unfathomable to our educated minds. Occasionally it actually seems to work. But inconsistency seems its biggest pitfall. Would that Hosteen Tso could eliminate the great water needs of his people so easily as he can satisfy the needs of Mr. Ford.

STATE OF THE NATION

In itself, Monument Valley is a rich concerto of fabulous color. But once he has succumbed to the magnificence and grandeur of the god-like sights all about him, the visitor finds that much of that color is found in the presence of the people of the Navajo nation who make the valley their home. Even after almost one hundred years of the white man's suppression, their rich heritage still domaintes their culture and remains master of all. Living habits for the vast majority have changed only slightly since the days before there was an invading hostile white man. The traveler in Monument Valley still can see the primitive homes and ancient customs of The People. He can admire the painstaking effort that is required in making rugs and silver products, and, if he is extremely lucky, he may even be able to witness the performance of a Yei-be-chai Dance, or a Squaw Dance, or perhaps even be present at a "sing" and watch the making of a sand painting. These things are all still very much a part of Navajo land, but what of the state of their nation as world progress surges about them?

In 1868, about 7,300 Navajos were released from Fort Sumner and allowed to return to their homelands. Add to this the number of Indians that remained free during the years of the imprisonment, and there was, perhaps, a total of 8,000 members in the Navajo tribes. Today that number stands at more than 61,000 — 12,000 families — a figure that shows clearly

Weathered sandstone formations

the fabulous rate of increase these people are able to maintain despite the many adverse conditions that result in a high infant mortality rate, as well as a high death rate caused by contagious diseases among the adults. The Navajo is our largest Indian tribe by far, and yet what has been done for these First Americans? What have we done for the proud descendants of Hoskinnini who still roam the valley of the monuments?

At Fort Sumner, when their freedom was granted, the Navajos stated: The Indians desire peace and now pledge their honor to keep it. It was agreed by The People that they would stay within the designated limits of the newly created reservation and would compel their children to attend school.

The United States promised that for every thirty children between the ages of six and thirteen who could be induced or compelled to attend school, a building would be provided and a teacher competent to teach the elementary branches of an English education would be furnished. This

Monument Valley in the winter
PHOTOGRAPHER UNKNOWN

person would reside among the Indians and faithfully discharge his or her duties as teacher. In 1947, with 22,000 children of school age on the reservation, facilities had been provided for five or six thousand. Since that date, little has been done to correct the deplorable situation as it existed then. Of the total population of the reservation, perhaps 20 per cent can speak English with any degree of fluency. A Navajo's chance of securing a job off the reservation is small indeed when he cannot even speak the language of his employers. Clearly the facts speak for themselves. We cannot be proud of the way in which we have kept our 1868 treaty. Still, if the Indians were to arise suddenly, and renew their long-dormant marauding tactics in retaliation for our neglect, we would at once condemn them as blood-thirsty savages.

Though the land they call home is striking in its enchantment and beauty, it is also striking with respect to its appalling lack of moisture. Water is always difficult to find and is forever a precious commodity. Meager supplies must be conserved and used with care. During drought years, such as 1950, many of the water sources dry up, heaping additional hardship and inconvenience upon the red man. For most of us, who need only to turn to the water faucet, it is hard to realize the true value of water. When Harry Goulding was drilling the well that now brings water to his lodge from five miles away, it was jokingly said that he might find gold, or strike oil. "God forbid!" said Harry. "I'd rather find water!"

Though there are about three hundred acres of land per person if it were to be divided up equally, that amount could not support a person at even a low level of subsistence. Following the return from the Bosque Redondo, both the Navajo and his flocks increased very rapidly. The general result was that, by 1930, their lands were so seriously overgrazed that large mesas, with the fertile topsoil eroded away, had become useless. Sheep and goats are especially destructive to the land they graze upon. Sheep, because of their mobile lips and their sharp incisor teeth, are particularly adapted for feeding on short grasses. With their pointed noses it is possible for them to crop the grasses down into the ground, thus killing the roots. In 1931, the number of sheep and goats was estimated to have reached an all-time high—nearly a million sheep and more than a third of a million goats. To prevent further deterioration of the Indian lands, the United States government stepped in and limited numbers. This resulted in reducing land destruction, but it also removed the chief economic prop of the tribe.

Over a period of years when the Indians' economy was at a perilous low ebb, successive flock reductions amounted to almost 25 per cent of the sheep and almost 70 per cent of the goats.

Even today it could truthfully be said that it is against the law for a Navajo to make a living. Everything is against him. His stock has been reduced in numbers, removing a part of his meager income, and adequate measures to teach him proper management of his remaining stock have not been undertaken. His land will scarcely support the animals he still has. If all projected irrigation and water-control projects were carried out— and they have not been—the entire reservation could serve the needs of perhaps 35,000 people. And yet, the population is close to double that figure. It takes thirty acres of land to support one sheep. It takes 150 to provide the necessary forage for a single horse, and 120 for each cow. If a person were to be allotted his hypothetical three hundred acres, he could have one sheep, one horse, and one cow. Indeed, a large herd! Added to this is the problem of water. A horse requires ten gallons every day. A sheep needs a gallon and a half. And still, the water supply is so meager. It has been remarked that Navajo sheep are the hardiest breed in the world. Actually, that is anything but remarkable. They have to be.

Statistics, dry as they may seem, speak loudly and stand for much in the Indian country. They continue to show, time after time, the regrettable status of the people. The normal per capita income (in 1940 it was $81.89 and remains about the same today) is less than one-tenth of the national average.

Navajo women earn from five to seventeen cents a day, designing and weaving their unique and beautiful rugs, a craft they learned about 1780, after imitating the loom of the Pueblo people and acquiring the wool from the Spaniards. At first they made only striped blankets for their own use, then later began trading the product to the Spanish colonists. The industry did not assume great importance until after the release from the Bosque Redondo, when their former ancestral domain was easily penetrated by outsiders. It was then that the traders induced the Navajos to make rugs instead of blankets. Zig-zag and diamond designs gained great popularity, replacing many of the earlier stripe patterns. All the weaving is done by the women and is processed from their own sheep. They keep the design in mind and develop it as they weave, starting from the bottom and working up. Halfway down, the rug is turned over and started at the bottom again, meeting the first half in the middle. No design is perfect, for if it were the gods might believe the weaver is striving for unearthly perfection, nor is any rug ever made without a loose end permitting escape of any evil spirits woven into the rug. And yet, for all this labor, a small saddle blanket, which takes from two to three months to weave, sells to the trader for perhaps eight or nine dollars at the most.

There are more than five thousand cases of tuberculosis on the reservation. The death rate from the disease is fourteen times greater than for the rest of the nation. Three out of every ten babies die at birth. Until very recently, medical attention for an Indian of the Monument Valley area was secured only at far-off Tuba City, one hundred miles to the southwest. The nearest resident doctor or dentist still is located there and all of six hospital beds are available to every thousand Indians. To reach Tuba the patient must be well enough to ride a horse or be fortunate enough to beg a ride from

Navajo woman spinning wool
PHOTOGRAPH BY ROY AND BROWNIE ADAMS

someone who owns a car. There is no public transportation system in the valley, nor anywhere else in the entire reservation.

This was the picture only a few short years ago. But since then a small bright star of hope has dawned over the red rocks and sands of Monument Valley. Early in 1951, Harry Goulding found success at the end of a long quest. In exchange for a small part of his land, the Seventh Day Adventist Church consented to Harry's request that a small school and medical clinic, in addition to a place of worship, be built there among the monuments. So, today, primary medical attention is offered just inside the Big Rock Door Canyon by the Elder and Mrs. Marvin Walter. And business is rushing. In the near future a small school will be ready to tackle the momentous job of initiating an education for the many Navajo youngsters of the valley.

And indeed that job is a tremendous one. There are 44,000 illiterates on the reservation. Nine out of every ten cannot read or write English. Even the minimum of our promised education certainly would result in more than one literate person out of every ten. Our shortcomings are all too obvious. Recently, at a place called Tolani, the only school for six hundred school-age children in that area was found to hold only sixty children. And it had been closed for five years because of lack of funds and teachers. In Monument Valley, there are no schools of any kind. Children from that area, 1,200 square miles, all must be taken out of the valley to boarding schools. With the severe shortage of educational facilities a certain amount of "valley pride" predominates and residents see to it that the Monument Valley youth are well represented in the classroom. So it is that Harry tells, with a rueful smile, of the "round-up" each fall when the jeeps go out into the valley and collect as many children as they can find. At the boarding schools in Dinnehotso and Chinle it's a clean-cut case of first come, first served. Those who arrive too late return home without their education for that year. Compare these facilities—teachers, buildings, and transportation— with those of our own school system.

True, there are problems that make the necessary schooling more difficult than a slight appraisal of the situation shows. The reservation has very little in the way of a satisfactory network of roads. Thus far, the Indian Service has allowed no oiled roads into the reservation. The only satisfactory and sure way to reach school, unless that school is a boarding school where the students stay throughout the entire school year, is by horseback. Because of the nature of the country many people are isolated from their neighbors.

Since the school buildings necessarily would have to be placed where the most people could reach them, some still would have far to go for their education. But if the instruction were there when they arrived, it would become most worthwhile to make the journey.

In the years just previous to World War II the government commenced

Traditional Navajo loom made from a juniper tree

PHOTOGRAPH BY ROY AND BROWNIE ADAMS

a planned course for improving the Indian lands. Springs and seeps were developed, a few retaining dams were built, and a number of public buildings were erected before the war broke out. During the war years that followed, all this activity naturally came to a halt, and has not been renewed.

But the picture is not all gloomy. In the postwar years much emphasis has been directed to the solution of the Navajo problem. Public attention is being directed to the Southwest as it never was before. A few improvements have been made, though completion of the needed projects apparently is far off. The current long-range Navajo policy embodies the principles of stock reduction, improved management, soil conservation, promotion of arts and crafts sales, water development, more practical education, a variety of small enterprises such as timber operation and canning projects, development of the Navajo leaders, and better farming methods. It is hoped that satisfactory progress in all these fields can be made in the near future. With the population of the reservation increasing yearly, improvements must come soon. Increased outside interest in such territories as Monument Valley means that Indian advancement must parallel external developments. Commercial and industrial exploitation, if it comes too suddenly, can wipe out all the advancements made by such men as Harry Goulding. Waves of unthinking tourists could too quickly recall the feeling of hostility toward all whites, a feeling not natural to these people, but still not forgotten from the last century.

The Navajo is vigorous, intelligent, and capable of hard work if it is not too continuous. Many times he will render assistance for the sake of friendship alone. He is loyal and cheerful when fairly treated. But he is also highly independent and will desert with scant ceremony when he has been treated unfairly. He can be trusted with valuable things and important missions. One caution, though. In many places it is considered bad taste to admit ignorance of the location of a certain place. Thus, rather than give no direction at all and be rude about the whole matter, the Indian will offer directions that are entirely products of his own imagination.

Examples of the complete "humanness" of The People are easy to find and striking in their sincerity. The Navajo is in remarkably close adjustment with his surroundings. Despite all hardships, he maintains a carefree outlook on life and the lack of his spontaneous good humor is rare indeed. And his considerations of others are always first. He will never camp close to a water source. He will remain in the vicinity but will set up camp perhaps a mile or two away, walking in for the water he needs. His reason is a generous one. If he were to camp closer, as any white man would, his presence would frighten away the wildlife of the vicinity which also needs the waterhole to survive.

Though basically a nomad, the Indian confines his wanderings to a more or less clearly defined section of land in which there is sufficient water and grazing land—more or less—for his needs. Other families respect the imaginary boundaries and trouble never arises. In drought years, when springs and seeps dry up, some families must share their supply. But there is never an argument over one of these affairs. A gentleman's agreement results, and without hostility the families "double up" and share their meager resources until such time as they are able to use their own water again. Are these happy and practical people the ones we call warlike and bloodthirsty?

Harry Goulding and Indians share a camp dinner

PHOTOGRAPH BY ROY AND BROWNIE ADAMS

A rough estimate of the cost of needed construction in all of the Navajo land is in the neighborhood of $1,000,000,000. In addition to this would be the cost of permanent maintenance of the developments. It seems a large figure. But consider it in the light of the intense need of these people. And consider it in respect to the nation's honor. At any price, we must back up our faithful promises of 1868.

A LOOK AHEAD

So much for the past and the present in Monument Valley. Now what of its future? The number of visitors is increasing annually, and in the years ahead this influx of tourists will present more and more of a problem. A problem that will have to be solved soon. Steps must be taken to see that this wonder of the world is preserved, not only for us but for the generations to come.

The problems involved in the fate of the enchanted valley are not new ones by any means. Representatives of the National Park Service of the Department of the Interior made a study of the Monument Valley area in March of 1931. The purpose of the investigation was to determine the suitability of the region for inclusion, along with other areas, in a then-proposed Navajo National Park. Of the lands that were to be included in this national park, Rainbow Bridge National Monument and Navajo National Monument were then, and still are, units of the National Park System.

Horace M. Albright, erstwhile exponent of the project (he established three other national parks and ten national monuments in his four years in office), was director of the Park Service at that time, having succeeded Stephen Mather, first Park Service director, who had retired in 1929. Albright was among those who made the trip into the valley of the monuments and, as everyone is, he was vastly impressed by the things he saw there. Standing at the base of one of the red rock monuments he expressed his belief that the valley they stood in would someday be considered one of the great wonders of the world.

On returning to Washington, the party issued a report of its findings. It contained this excerpt:

"Monument Valley. This area lies partly in Arizona and partly in Utah. There are many detached mesas, buttes, and slender, towering pinnacles that are the products of heavy erosion over a large area. These 'monuments' have a weird and unreal appearance. The area is highly scenic, unique, interesting, and unlike any existing national park. Most of the formations are brilliantly red in color. The area is arid and vegetation is of the desert type."

Concerning the proposed national park the report stated:

"The area is of such outstanding scenic quality that it would be an important addition to the National Park system. The scenery is varied, full of interest, and is of impressive magnitude. Monument Valley, Tsagi Canyon, Navajo Canyon, Rainbow Bridge and its vicinity, are among the spectacular scenic features of the area."

The proposed Navajo National Park had the backing of the local people at that time. One of the more ardent supporters of the proposal was Mr. Emil Gammeter, a state representative in the Utah state legislature. Practically all the lands involved were absorbed into the Navajo Reservation when the Piute strip was added in March of 1933.

At first it was believed that a satisfactory agreement could be worked out with the Navajos. But when the proposal to establish a national park was taken up with the Navajo Tribal Council, it was vigorously opposed and no mutually satisfactory agreement could be reached. Because of this opposition and the complicated land status, the proposal was side-channelled and has since been dormant.

From that date, though nothing has been committed officially, the place of the monuments has been discussed repeatedly as a federal preserve in its own right, as it certainly should be. A more comprehensive plan suggests that the valley be included in one gigantic national park that would sweep across the Escalante country of Utah and include all its many wonders. From Arches National Monument and the Fisher Towers on the north, south along the Colorado to include Natural Bridges, Monument Valley, Rainbow Bridge, and perhaps a number of others, this huge national park would embrace some of our nation's most outstanding wonders, finally tying in with Grand Canyon National Park on the southern end. Monument Valley needs and deserves the protection we can give it. Though its final destiny is out of our hands, we can assist in the preservation of its wonder and mystery for those of our generations.

If the valley were to be set aside as a national park, that is, if the Indians were to permit its establishment, it is quite probable that they would be forced out of it. Such has been the case in other national parks, Grand Canyon to name only one. Park Service policy prevents the private exploitation of lands that come under its control, and rightly so in the vast majority of cases. But here there is a different sort of problem. The Navajo people would suddenly be deprived of a large portion of their limited and sparse grazing lands, lands that even now are not sufficient to take care of their needs.

However, if the area remains uncontrolled it soon will be damaged materially by the over-zealous and inconsiderate tourist. Noteworthy, as one

"Mike" and Harry Goulding with their tour car, 1930s. Note the trading post logo on the car door

PHOTOGRAPHER UNKNOWN

browses through the place of the red rock monuments, is that there is a gladdening and surprising lack of discarded tires, empty bottles, and rusting tin cans along the roadside; and the usual names and addresses have not yet been carved into the soft sandstone of the monuments.

For the most part, Monument Valley is just as God made it, just as He intended it to be. But for how long will it remain that way? Thus far, all white visitors into the valley have been largely under the personal guidance of Harry Goulding, the one-man protective society of the valley. Meeting and photographing the Indians becomes an intimate affair in each case. Almost every person who goes there tends to depart with a sincere understanding of The People.

But there is an increasing number of those who reach into the valley on their own, in Jeeps, or other low-geared vehicles. Already the Careless One is invading Monument Valley and tarnishing the virgin touch found there. Poncho House, once a splendid ruin on the northwest edge of the valley has been sacked and all but ruined. Honeymoon Cottage, a tiny Indian ruin huddled beneath splendid Wedding Ring Arch in Mystery Valley rested undisturbed for six hundred years. Just recently it was destroyed by a man of little heart. The pristine nature of this land can so easily be destroyed if we become thoughtless and careless.

So the problem at hand is quite obvious. With federal control, the Indians could be forced out. Without it, he soon will be overrun and his scenic home rudely degraded. If the National Park Service comes into the valley it must come armed with special legislation which permits the red man to remain undisturbed. All the present color can be retained only if the Navajo is permitted to stay. He should continue to own his land. We should come only to gaze on its wonders, and leave no trace of our visit. And federal protection must be gained or these matchless wonders will be forever lost.

THE ENCHANTED VALLEY

The moment you enter into the magic land of Monument Valley you realize that there is some of the eternal there. There is something Godly and everlasting that strikes to the very bottom of your soul. And for tens of thousands of years this land has remained almost the same. Today, as it was through a thousand generations, it remains a monument to God. From no matter where you come you'll find something truly spiritual in Monument Valley. Drowsing in warm sunshine or full of fury in the face of a desert thunderstorm it seems to be a land where yesterday is, somehow, more permanent that today. It is a part of another world—one you never have visited. To go there you must cross a million miles and wing your way through a hundred thousand years to where time has faded and become nothing. That is the everlasting way of Monument Valley. It clings about your heart and burrows deep inside. It is, all at once, impossible to realize that other lands exist. Only this seems real, while our noisy street cars and buses, our hollow structures of metal and stone, our petty human attempts at greatness seem to be far away, or perhaps, never to have existed at all.

Yet, the time-and-space bridge into the valley of the monuments is one of the mind and heart only. Actually you can reach the valley quite easily. North, south, east, and west, where well-travelled Indian trails once circled a quiet land, the land of the Navajos, are modern highways of concrete and macadam over which cars and trucks dash energetically, intent upon their frail human purpose. On the west, U. S. Highway 89 leaves Flagstaff, Arizona, at the foot of the giant San Francisco Peaks and goes directly northward into Utah, barely brushing the reservation from Cameron to the Utah state line. Highway 66 provides a southern border to Indian land, but never once actually touches the Navajo country. U. S. Highway 666 cuts the eastern reaches of the reservation, but to the north, paved highway 160 does not approach closer than about one hundred miles to the preserve itself.

Enclosed within this border of paving is an area that remains wild and largely untouched. These are virgin lands, though a part of the white man's domain for several hundreds of years. Probably there is no section of land of comparable size in the United States that belongs more completely to you, as a citizen, than the lands of northern Arizona and southern Utah. Eighty per cent of this land is government-owned. Grand Canyon, Bryce Canyon, and Zion—the national parks: Cedar Breaks, Capitol Reef, Arches, Natural Bridges, Hovenweep, Navajo, Wupatki, Sunset Crater, Walnut Canyon, Petrified Forest, Canyon de Chelly—the national monuments, all set aside to preserve areas of outstanding beauty and interest. National forests and Indian reservation lands also are government-owned, with you as direct heir. In the heart of this mammoth panorama of magnificence rests Monument Valley.

And the roads that take you into it are your personal call to high and

Monument Valley panorama
PHOTOGRAPH BY GIBBS M. SMITH

unequalled adventure. They guide you into the exciting realm of never-never. In all honesty the intra-reservation roads should not be identified by that name at all. Perhaps the name has been given to them in a burst of diabolical humor. Rather, there should be a special designation for them. One that implies their real meaning, both as to condition and romantic appeal.

Yet, these roads of shifting sand and slick rock are the only way you can reach into Monument Valley by automobile. This is the land where the sure-footed horse and burro are the unrivaled kings of transportation. Only on horseback can you find that lack of responsibility and freedom from restraint that allows the hardy adventurer to answer the call of the unknown and find awesome things of wonder and magnitude such as he never could have conjured up in his imagination. But the roads are passable, and nothing more is necessary. They keep the fainthearted away, and those who are afraid have no place there in the land that is so rich and so beautiful.

That land you go into breathes and pulsates with strange fascination and mystery. The excellent book, *The Inverted Mountains,* edited by Roderick Peattie, says: "The roads are a bit better than going across country, but respect those who think otherwise. Don't plan on arriving any place at a certain time. If the roads don't get you, the scenery will. Either way, there will be several stops!" Even the very names of the settlements are strangely exciting in Indian land. Your tongue soon learns to curl around such names as Dinnehotso, Tes Nos Pas, Lukachukai, and somehow there is great pleasure in merely repeating them to others. They bear the real flavor of this mysterious land—difficult and often hard to pronounce, yet full of romance and sounding rich in unexcelled adventure.

The valley of the monuments can be reached from the north and from the south by a single continuous road that leaves paved Highway 89 just north of Cameron, Arizona, and sagely winds its way across mesa and desert for over two hundred miles, until, surprisingly enough, it comes out at Blanding, and later meets concrete again at Monticello, Utah. Either entrance provides an exciting method of approach. And inasmuch as the road is continuous, it provides a method for entering and leaving the valley without retracing your steps. The true adventurer can find variations on the road that eventually lead into Monument Valley, but unless he is well-versed in the ways of desert driving and has an automobile of sufficient clearance and powerful enough to enable him to pull through drifted sand, he will be wise to stay on what is loosely termed the main road. Even then, he is lucky if forward motion is not stopped occasionally, calling for the application of muscle power.

Driving in the desert is an experience very new to most casual visitors to the region. Consequently, there is need for great care and caution. It is absolutely necessary that a shovel be carried at all times when travelling through the reservation. Often, the mere presence of that shovel seems to discourage the car from getting stuck. But when wheels do spin and dig deep into the red dust, it is wise, and most certainly time-saving, to have a long-handled shovel tied conveniently behind the front bumper. Several wooden planks also may be carried to good advantage, providing a means of traction if the car gets stuck. Low-pressure tires pull out more rapidly and more regularly than do the standard high-pressure tires. If wheels should remain buried, it is best to lower the air pressure, thus giving the tires more surface area, and increased traction. For this it is necessary to

Sun shines through a hole in the roof of a sandstone cave

PHOTOGRAPH BY RONALD W. HARRIS

Petroglyphs in Mystery Valley
PHOTOGRAPH BY RONALD W. HARRIS

carry an air pump in the car so that tires may be returned to their normal pressure once the trouble spot has been passed.

Though you may have these items on hand in your car you will not necessarily be called upon to use them. But their mere presence is most comforting. Usually the main roads into Monument Valley are quite easily crossed. Only after a prolonged period of dryness, when the sand becomes powdery, or after a severe rain, when portions of the road have been washed away, is there any real danger. And even then, it usually can be avoided through care. Never let fear of desert driving discourage you from entering upon the great adventure that awaits you just inside of Navajo land. But tackle the job wisely. Talk with others who know desert driving and find from them the real hazards that may occur. Stop frequently to ask questions of the white traders on the reservation for they know the roads intimately.

Though there is endless dust, little water, and the roads are always rough, you'll be rewarded with a great prize that more than repays your efforts. Dust will brush off, you can carry adequate water with you, and the rough road can safely be navigated and is soon passed, but the fantasy that is Monument Valley never can be erased from your memory.

From the southwest, the semimaintained road, which eventually reaches Monument Valley and goes north to Mexican Hat and Bluff, leaves U. S. Highway 89 at a point nine miles north of Cameron, Arizona. Before that, even from the very moment you leave Flagstaff, it is easy and right to fill your imagination with the valley and wonderings of what it will be like. And yet you cannot guess because it is forever different. The monuments and the buttes remain unchanged, but even as they do, the sun and clouds play weird tricks with them, inviting you to return again and again to see the game that Nature is playing today .

When you have left the blue San Franciscos behind, and have crossed the Coconino divide, passing from the shadows of the tall ponderosa pines that surround the Flagstaff area, anticipation of Monument Valley becomes even greater. Crossing the Little Colorado River at Cameron means entrance to the reservation. This is the borderline where the red man drinks Coca-Cola and looks in aloofness at the white man's strange and so-called civilized ways, and where the white man buys Navajo workmanship and wonders when, if ever, the Indian will evolve from his savage pattern. Two great and opposing cultures meet, with little of absorption on either side.

Where the Monument Valley road turns off to the right, the traveller finds himself immediately confronted by a sign that needs only a skull and crossbones to make its threat complete.

Road conditions from here on are
uncertain and often hazardous.
TRAVEL AT YOUR OWN RISK

Note it carefully because it does give fair warning, but do not turn back. Only the faint of heart stop there—those who would not enjoy Monument Valley, nor understand its religion.

The country is arid and without hint or suggestion of vegetation. This is the northern edge of the Painted Desert and the lack of greens is made up for by the presence of a host of other colors. Passing between Moenkopi and Kaibito plateaus, you travel gently from one era into another. Since leaving Flagstaff you have covered generations in space and time. Tuba City, the first settlement that consists of anything more than a trading post, is a true study in contrasts. It lies in the middle of the surrounding desolation and yet it is a veritable oasis of green. Tuba clearly indicates the difference between the presence of water and the lack of it, the narrow line between life and death in this land where only the fittest have survived.

All that leads up to Monument Valley is a true crescendo, always growing in its intensity. Twenty miles northeast of Tuba City is Tonalea, a typical Indian trading post. It consists only of a group of buildings that indicates a white trader who can speak to the traveller in English and knows of the road conditions ahead. At Tonalea the country still is made up largely of sand and rock, those criteria of the Indian lands, with very little in the way of trees or shrubs. This trading post is located in the heart of the rug-weaving country, where Navajo rugs of beautiful color and intricate pattern are a matter of course.

To the west can be seen White Mesa, with its hidden canyons and tortuous washes. Difficult to reach except with pack animals, White Mesa, identified by its coloring, is a veritable gold mine of ancient cliff-dwelling ruins—ruins that have barely been scratched by archaeologists and other scientists. It seems hard to believe that within sight of the road lies a region, parts of which have never been travelled across and examined by the inquisitive white man. But you must become accustomed to believing the impossible. Far ahead lies the land of room enough and time enough where anything is possible.

Tonalea formerly was identified as Red Lake, but because of an over-abundance of Red Lakes at other points on the reservation, this one had its name changed to Tonalea. A small lake, red in appearance, caused by the color of the surrounding soil, appears intermittently in a basin below the trading post, and gave the post its original name. This is a United States post office, but service necessarily is limited. Mail comes in on Mondays and Fridays, goes out on Tuesdays and Saturdays. It's another signpost to tell you that hurry is out of place in Indian land. There's always plenty of time to do everything. The man who drives the mail truck has a route that leads him farther from a railroad than any other point in the United States—John Wetherill's Kayenta.

Six miles north of Tonalea a road turns off to the left, heading for Rainbow Lodge and the unforgettable two-day pack trip to gemlike Rainbow Bridge. From this junction you still can turn and look south to see the San Francisco Peaks almost one hundred miles away. As they fade on the horizon they signal the departure of another world—one you knew but no longer have any part of. Already you are living the enchantment of new lands.

Three miles beyond the Rainbow Bridge road, the main road branches a second time, the left fork leading to Shonto and, eventually, Navajo National Monument. Unless you crave an unforgettable but time-consuming adventure, wait until you have gone twenty-three miles farther along the main road, then turn west on the improved road to the monument. That one assures you of getting there. The other one dares you. It attempts to surmount a number of barriers, and, although *it* succeeds, *you* may not be so fortunate until after a repeated number of tries.

Approaching Shonto Springs, the road descends a long slope, consisting largely of loose sand, then crosses a stream without benefit of a bridge. For its crowning achievement, the road makes a supreme effort to climb the face of a cliff at what would appear to be greater than a forty-five degree angle. This is the so-called slick-rock at its best. The road has been hewn out of the living rock without thought as to comfortable passage. The moment there was any chance that the ascent could be made, all construction was halted and never resumed. The result means a simple but lengthy driving procedure that proceeds thus: Creep along in low gear while all four wheels of the car hit different bumps at the same time. Fortunately there is no traffic and you can take your time—a rather doubtful and ludicrous benefit since you have no choice. When the motor gasps, gives a last cough, and dies, wait for the vapor-lock to go away, then try all over again. Another hundred yards is gained by repeating the same actions. In the hour it takes you to climb one mile you will have gained a most intimate and detailed knowledge of the surrounding country.

Just north of the turnoff to Shonto Springs is the approved road to Navajo National Monument, and just beyond that lies Marsh Pass. There, red and brown outcroppings of sandstone are the forerunners of Monument Valley. A roadside marker—an extreme rarity along this road—identifies the pass. It is only fifteen miles from Kayenta, the last settlement until you reach Mexican Hat, some sixty miles from the pass. The Monument Valley-Rainbow Bridge expeditions discovered and examined several fine ruins in the region of Marsh Pass.

Kayenta is the post that was founded by John Wetherill and operated by him until his death, in 1949. It marks the end of the mail route, the end of the single telephone line that has been hugging the road since you left the black-topped highway many miles back, and just about the beginning of Monument Valley. At Kayenta, there is a junction with a road that has struggled all the way from Shiprock, New Mexico, passing through Mexican Water and Dinnehotso. For the adventurer who may have enjoyed the climb at Shonto, there is a stretch of fifteen miles of similar road to tackle before reaching Mexican Water. Fifteen miles of slick-rock that takes two to two and one-half hours to cross!

From Kayenta, the road dips into a deep wash, climbs again to the desert floor, then heads directly into the base of Agathlan, the giant 1,225-foot volcanic spire that contrasts so vividly with the surrounding country. But just before reaching the black lava plug, the road curves gently to the left, passing between Agathlan and Owl Rock.

On first view, the rugged black peak of Agathlan appears impossible to climb, and a closer inspection apparently confirms this impression, but on May 29 and 30, 1949, the first ascent *was* made. Three young men completed their breathless adventure, then later left this account in Harry Goulding's guest book: "Climbed black dike on N.W. to contact summit ridge. Used 40 pitons and one tamp-in bolt for protection. No direct aid. Total time from base of cliff to return—25 hours. Spent night on peak." Almost a classic in brevity.

Owl Rock is absurd. It shouldn't be there at all. Passive and unconcerned it sits there on the plateau across from Agathlan, glaring down at each passer-by. It is the first of the monuments, your first real clue as to what Monument Valley will be like. The owl can be recognized just as the road passes directly by him. It's a great guardian, massive and silent in this land of the monuments, where massiveness and silence stand supreme.

From the north, which may be the way of exit from Monument Valley when entrance has been made through Tuba City, Tonalea, and Kayenta, the road into the place of the monuments leaves Highway 160 at the Mormon town of Monticello, Utah. An all-weather road leads into Blanding, another town of the Mormons. From Blanding, gravel extends south for thirteen miles, then peters out and sand takes over for the rest of the way into the valley. Approaching Bluff, the road crosses a corner of Sage Plain, which extends eastward into Colorado, then leaves the plateau and descends to the valley of the San Juan River, through Cow Canyon. The valley there is wide and flat, with bluffs rising again to the south, on the opposite side of the river. Bluff itself, a patch of green, has never equalled the peak population of 225 people that it once held. Today it boasts no more, but only sleeps in the sun. Before oil was discovered in Mexican Hat at the turn of the present century, Bluff was the end of the line. But when the black gold began to flow, even in meager amounts, a road was carved through from the Hat.

From Bluff, the road climbs steep-sided Comb Ridge—the same ragged ridge that later forms the eastern border of Monument Valley—passes across its summit, and descends on the western slope. From there the road wends its way for a mile through Snake Canyon, amidst eroded red hills and said to be so named when an unfortunate snake broke its back in crawling through it. West of Snake Canyon the road climbs again, crossing brush-covered Lime Ridge, and from this high point may be seen the first breathtaking view of Monument Valley. On the horizon, faint purple spires, buttes, and mesas loom skyward and lure you on to their shadowed enchantment.

View looking west across Mystery Valley. Navajo Mountain can be seen faintly in the background

PHOTOGRAPH BY GIBBS M. SMITH

A few miles farther on the main road passes a side road which leads to the overlook of the Goosenecks of the San Juan, a truly impressive sight, and one of the world's most magnificent examples of the "entrenched meander." To achieve an airline distance of but a single mile the river makes three great successive loops totaling six miles. The canyon walls are more than twelve hundred feet high at this point and provide a breathtaking view in a land where outstanding views are around every corner.

Mexican Hat is the last white settlement in Utah, on the road south into the valley. There the road crosses the San Juan for the first time, accomplishing that feat via a suspension bridge that groans ominously at every vehicular crossing. The bridge is due to be replaced during 1953 with a newer, more trustworthy, structure. It is from Mexican Hat that J. Frank Wright takes adventure seekers down the San Juan and Colorado rivers for 191 miles of excitement in his specially constructed boats. And it is easy to see why the take-off from the embarking point close to the bridge provides the first of many thrills.

The rock strata at this point are inclined slightly upward, being higher in the west than in the east. Also, the brownish-green waters of the San Juan, though not particularly rough here, seem to be hurrying beneath the bridge on their way downhill. The combination of the uptilted rocks and the river that seems to be going downhill succeeds in giving an illusion that is dispelled only after the boats have been pushed into the water and it is discovered that the picture is not as bad as it was thought to be.

Norman Nevills formerly operated these adventure trips until both he and his wife were killed in a plane crash in 1949. It seems ironical that a man who fought the San Juan and the Colorado to a standstill should die such an opposing death. But he left a worthy successor in Frank Wright. The adventure remains the same—as thrilling as ever.

From the suspension bridge at the Hat, the road winds its way up a steep cliff affording many outstanding views of the San Juan and its valley. Again, from the top of the mesa, you can see to the south the strangely fascinating and unreal land of the monuments. The closer your approach, the more you wonder if perhaps this is not all a dream. Still, who could dream of such wonderful things as these? Somewhere, somehow, there has to be an inspiration, even to dreams. And in Monument Valley it is spread before you, to give inspiration to your life and dreams.

It is in this respect that the northern approach actually rivals the one coming in from the south. Down from Bluff the valley lures you onward. Every new view increases in fascination until finally you are there among the monuments, actually breathing the air of enchantment. From the south, the traveller is left to grasp the sudden immensity of the situation without fair prelude to its mightiness. Rounding Owl Rock he is asked to look upon a great portion of the valley all at once. The result is overwhelming. It is better to let the greatness creep over you slowly—as it must if you but linger there awhile.

A few more miles and a slight climb takes the southbound road up through Monument Pass, so called because it is bordered on both sides by the monuments. From the pass, purpled with distance far to the west, may be seen the Clay Hills, Train Rock, and the Henry Mountains. Then follows the descent into the valley, where all the grandeur and magic is yours, to hold in your heart and soul.

Adjectives and words of description flow easily when you have seen Monument Valley, but for the most part they seem useless—frustratingly inadequate when it comes to the telling. Mere words can never do justice to anything which has the marvel and magnitude, the grandeur and glory, of the place of the monuments. In both words and paints there have been many who have tried to capture its romance, but none who have truly succeeded. Each word-picture only begins to stir up the mental image that should be Monument Valley.

Charles L. Bernheimer, writing of the 1921 expedition made to Rainbow Natural Bridge, by the American Museum of Natural History, makes this recording of his impression of Monument Valley: "Looking east from Navajo Mountain the sunset was a marvel of color. Monument Valley lay before us, three thousand feet below. Each visible monument, and there seemed to be no end of them, glowed in an orange-red fire, each bordered on its easterly face by a strongly contrasting blue-slate shadow. The monuments looked like shooting jets of fire, their purple-grey shadows like smoke."

Certainly everyone who has ever dreamed, and peered into the valley of the monuments, discovers that a dream has come true. And always it burrows into his soul and results in heroic attempts at description. Certainly there is in the country a vastness, power, and vivid eternal peace that affects each visitor. Irvin S. Cobb threw geologic theory to the winds when he called the Monument Valley-Rainbow Bridge area the place "where Old Marster stacked it up and scooped it out and shuffled it together again so violently, so completely, and with such incredibly beautiful tonings, such incomparable beautiful results."

Zane Grey once referred to the valley as a "yellow-and-purple corrugated world of distance." He mentions it again in his book, *Tales of Lonely Trails,* when he tells of a 1913 trip in which he visited the valley of the monuments with John Wetherill and was at once overwhelmed by its beauty.

"My first sight of Monument Valley came with a dazzling flash of lightning. It revealed a vast valley, a strange world of colossal shafts and buttes of rock, magnificently sculptured, standing isolated and aloof, dark, weird, and lonely. When the sheet lightning flared across the sky showing the

Monument Valley vista

PHOTOGRAPH BY ROBERT Z. BRUCKMAN

monuments silhouetted black against that strange horizon, the effect was marvelously beautiful. I watched until the storm died away.

"Dawn, with the desert sunrise, changed Monument Valley, bereft it of its night glow and weird shadow and showed it in another aspect of beauty. It was hard for me to realize that those monuments were not the works of man. The great valley must have been a plateau of red rock from which the softer strata has eroded, leaving the gentle league-long slopes marked here and there by upstanding pillars and columns of singular shape and beauty. I rode down the sweet-scented sage slopes under the shadow of the lofty Mittens and around and across the valley. And when I had completed my ride a story had woven itself into my mind; and the spot where I stood was to be the place where Lin Slone taught Lucy Bostil to ride the great stallion Wildfire."

On his return home, Grey produced *Desert Treasure* and *The Light of Western Stars* trying to recapture the experiences he had encountered on his trip through the fabulous lands of northern Arizona.

The late Ernie Pyle, famed columnist, visited the valley in 1939, and immediately was impressed with its grandeur. In a series of subsequent articles he eagerly betrayed his new-found love and told why it had been born.

There have been others who have fallen in love with the charm of the valley. The rare exception is the person who does not. In Harry Goulding's guest book are the names of hundreds of visitors who felt a deep inward touching of the soul when they visited Monument Valley. Their words are always the same, because there is no better way to express it. "Magnificent," "Wonderful," "Unbelievable"—all vague and futile attempts at describing the mysterious attraction that is forever there. But inevitably they always say, "We'll be back again." Henry Fonda said it that simply when he visited the valley for the filming of "My Darling Clementine." "I'll be back," he wrote, and he meant it. George O'Brien, Victor McLaglen, Dick Foran, Ward Bond, Pedro Armendariz, Grant Withers, John Agar, John Wayne— all famous names in that world of play-acting—all awed by the real life drama of Monument Valley.

Jack Breed, Neil Clark, Joyce and Josef Muench, Jimmy Swinnerton— other names in a book that records visitors to the place of the monuments. Add *your* name there beside the others.

Somehow, some of the truest expressions of the romance that is Monument Valley come in the person of its king. To know Harry Goulding is to find an immediate liking for him. He is one of those people with whom friendship comes easily, and you'll feel all the richer for having met and talked with him. Nor is meeting Harry anything of a problem. He's always there in the heart of Monument Valley, waiting for your visit. After spending a few hours, or preferably a few days or a week with him, and witnessing his strong devotion and love of the valley of the monuments I'm sure you'll agree that if Monument Valley were to be called a concerto of color and beauty, the presence of Harry Goulding has added delightful lyrics to it.

He is full of the interesting stories and tales that have come his way during the twenty-six years of his valley residence. He speaks the difficult Navajo language fluently and can wait just as long, and be just as patient as any red man. He refuses to carry a watch. Why should he? There's never a need for hurry in Monument Valley. The only things that go by schedule, and no one has ever regretted the exceptions, are the meals at the lodge. Breakfast at eight, lunch at twelve noon, dinner at six, unless the day's expedition has not returned. Harry always used to bellow "supper's ready" when that meal was on the table. But the ranch has grown up now. It's bigger and there are more people around, so it's easier and less of a strain to beat the old steel triangle that hangs by the dining room door. Everyone knows it's wise to answer that call, too. Appetites are forever at their peak in the dry air of Monument Valley, and a table loaded with the most delicious food to be found anywhere is a most welcome sight indeed.

Mail might lie unnoticed for several days if there are more important things to be done. Once when he was asked why he never brought a telephone into the valley Harry replied, "Mister, I'd shoot the man who put one of those things on my wall." You'll rarely hear a radio in Monument Valley either. The outside world quickly loses all importance when you have entered the valley of enchantment.

The thing that Harry quite apparently likes to do best, and continues to do with unabated enthusiasm, is to take his visitors into what he calls the "real Monument Valley." He does it with such joy and satisfaction that you feel he would leave without you, and go alone if necessary, just to see his valley in another of her moods. For most certainly, it is *his* valley. There is no deed to ownership outside of his one-mile square at the base of Tsay-Kizzi Mesa, but when you have travelled with Harry through the area that has the highest concentration of wonders, his "real Monument Valley," you'll

Navajo family in the 1940s
PHOTOGRAPHER UNKNOWN

know that if love has anything to do with it, Harry owns Monument Valley and all its people. He's always a bit disappointed by people who hurry through the valley unseeing and unthinking. One morning we noticed a cloud of dust out on the main road, speeding along the valley floor toward the north and Monument Pass. "What's that?" I asked.

Replied Harry: "That's probably some darn fool who *thinks* he's seeing Monument Valley."

The trip among the monuments is made in sturdy station wagons with powerful four-wheeled drive. It's been said that Harry and his Jeeps never know when to quit—they just keep right on going until the front wheels start to float. And I'm inclined to believe that's a statement quite near to the truth. In the past several years, with a pair of the loyal Jeeps, Harry has been able to penetrate farther into the back country than he ever found possible before. The Jeeps make their own roads and seem to derive a fiendish, "jeepish," delight in doing so. They apparently learn to thrive on loose sand and sagebrush. Any ordinary car would bog down immediately on leaving the main road. The four-wheeled drive station wagons take it all in stride.

The trip starts about nine in the morning and takes anywhere from eight to ten hours to complete. It all depends on how eager Harry is for you to see some particular sight at a special time of the day. If you have picture-taking equipment along (and be sure you do), he'll go far out of his way to provide you with pictures that will thrill the family members you left at home. It's a day full of sights that are unbelievably wonderful. It's a whole day spent among the buttes and mesas, the slender spires and balanced rocks, arches and bridges, ancient cliff dwellings, and natural wonders that are too impossible to believe.

The Mittens are the first great wonder. Like two gigantic hands they point skyward, silent and omnipotent. According to the Navajos, the Mittens are the Big Hands, signs of a great power that was once present upon earth, but is now dormant and still. One day, they say, the power will return again, to rule from Monument Valley. Not far from the Mittens is Merrick Butte where the old prospector saw his dreams of wealth and fortune vanish in the smoke of his campfire. Meridian Butte, to the northeast, is located on the 110th meridian.

Passing through the North Window into Superstition Valley, Harry tells the story of Old Cly, the Navajo whose name rests on the butte to the left.

Cly was a venerated chieftain who lived in the valley until his death, in 1934. When he passed away, they buried him at the foot of Cly Butte. True to Indian custom, they took all his possessions and "knocked them in the head" so that their spirits would go along with the chief. His horse was killed, as were his sheep, goats, and cattle, and his saddle and bridle were cut up and left there.

To the southwest are the saintly Three Sisters, another fantastic study in stone that takes only a little clarification before its obvious significance is clear. Harry knows all the Monuments by heart. Indeed, he has helped to name many of them. As the day passes—always all too quickly—he'll point out a submarine, sourdough biscuits, profiles of many people, and likenesses of every kind of animal. He'll show you any number of formations fashioned through the centuries by the tireless wind and rain.

Beyond the Three Sisters lies the Valley of Tsay-begi, the "Valley Within the Rocks," that fascinated Ernie Pyle when he visited there in 1939. The tiny valley, basking in warm sunshine, seems thoroughly imbued with legend, as a part of the past you never can touch. There is mystery in the Valley of Tsay-begi, a mystery of creation, a mystery of a glorious past.

Leaving the "Valley Within the Rocks" the Jeep goes by the Big Eye and the fabulous Ear of the Wind. Around the corner from the Ear is Echo Cave Ruin, a remnant of the Anasazi. Standing quietly in Echo Cave, and

Mittens

PHOTOGRAPHER UNKNOWN

then suddenly shouting a word or phrase, you will be amazed—and delighted —to hear from eight to sixteen separate echoes, the number depending upon the weather.

If time permits, you may be able to visit Hidden Bridge Canyon to the east and see the hidden bridge that so carefully conceals itself there. But the real climax to the day's journey is the Yei-bi-chai formation at the northern tip of Yei-bi-chai Mesa. The Totem Pole is the most obvious member of the Yei-bi-chai formation, and you won't believe it until you see it. More loudly than all the rest it shouts the question "why?" Why was it left standing? And why does it continue to stand there alone and unsupported, oblivious to its defiance of the laws that declare it should be sprawled and broken on the valley floor? Certainly it is easy to throw geologic theory aside here. More rightly, this must have been the feat of a raging barefooted creator who completed his work in a burst of enthusiasm with the designing

View of Rooster Rock, Meridian Butte, and the Yei Bi Chai Group

PHOTOGRAPH BY RONALD W. HARRIS

of the Totem Pole, and then stumbled over the paint pots, turning them upside down in his exit.

It's a day well invested, that day you go into the "real Monument Valley." It's one you'll long remember—but who would find it possible ever to forget the valley of the monuments?

In shape, Monument Valley is triangular, with Comb Ridge bounding it from northeast to southwest, No Man's Mesa along the southwestern and western sides, and the San Juan River the boundary marker on the north. The floor of the valley is a dome, rising gradually from 4,800 feet in Gypsum Valley to 5,200 feet at Monument Pass.* It then slopes gently to the west to the 4,800-foot elevation of upper Moonlight Valley. The monuments vary from spires to broad mesas with several miles of flat-topped caps. The igneous peaks, such as Alhambra and Agathlan, afford a striking contrast with the redness that is peculiar to the valley area. But though the geology may vary, the weather provides a perfect example of consistency.

Northern Arizona is estimated, on the average, to have 210 clear days, 85 partly cloudy, and 70 cloudy during a single year. Probably the clouds are even more rare in Monument Valley, where days of glory and nights of splendor are quite the rule. Rainfall amounts to about eight inches yearly, with the largest portion of the moisture coming in sudden and brief storms which may last a few hours or a few minutes. The soil is quickly drenched to a depth of about one inch and the rest becomes runoff. Hailstorms occur with enough regularity to be classed as fairly common. Due to the nature of the precipitation, one area may be caught in the pangs of a severe drought, while another area, only a few miles away, receives repeated drenchings. Snow frequently falls during the winter months at all valley elevations above five thousand feet. But its life is one of brevity. Giving a white cap of reverence to the monuments, it lingers but a few moments, then fades.

Despite the apparent lack of water, there is considerable wildlife in the area. Rabbits, prairie dogs, coyotes, trade rats, field mice, several species of snakes, a large variety of lizards, brown squirrels, and desert chipmunks all are quite common. The poisonous rattlesnake, though present in the valley, is rarely seen. The desert chipmunk, with his tail arched arrogantly up over his back, provides one of the most amusing sights. As much

* Arthur A. Baker, "Geology of the Monument Valley-Navajo Mountain Region, San Juan County, Utah," U.S.G.S. Survey *Bulletin* 865, Plate II, Washington, 1936, shows elevation of Monument Pass to be 5,600-5,700 feet.

intrigued by you as you are by him, he waits until the last minute to make
his retreat from your path, then often falls over himself in doing so.

A place of many moods, Monument Valley never twice appears to be
the same. There is not only seasonal, but daily, even hourly, change in the
place of the monuments. Mischievous lights and shadows play strange tricks,
racing over the color scale and producing every possible tint from flaming

Sandstone monolith

PHOTOGRAPH BY RONALD W. HARRIS

Seventh-Day Adventist mission hospital, 1960
PHOTOGRAPHER UNKNOWN

red to deep purple on the eternal monuments. Under moonlight, in storm, bearing a stately mantle of snowy-white, there is always something magnificently new, and yet so familiar and friendly about Monument Valley. Never is it cold or impersonal.

In springtime, just after a storm has passed, the valley abounds in growth, and appears as a great departure from its usual arid state. Many varieties of wild flowers grow suddenly in the soil that is rich when given water. There is mile after mile of blue lupine. Brilliant red pincushion and beavertail cactus blossoms, and yellow and pink yucca all gladden the face of the desert. Thousand-foot waterfalls cascade from the slick-rock mesas. Nature smiles and laughs—then her joyousness is ended. After a few hours of wild abandon and happiness the valley returns to its peaceful sumber.

The proper season for visiting the valley amounts to about twelve months out of every year. Rarely is there a disagreeable day, though March may be a bit too windy to suit your tastes. But visit the valley at any time and you'll be enthralled by a performance of nature that leaves you gasping. The most perfect period, though perfect seems a highly unnecessary superlative when every season is so splendid, is September and October, when skies are their very brightest and clouds are at their fluffy best. Nights have a nip, causing the blood to race and the spirits to soar skyward after the monuments. Then the camera enthusiast can enjoy himself to his heart's content. Nowhere can you discover skies that are bluer—or find clouds that are of more perfect whiteness than in the valley of the monuments. It is a photographer's paradise every day of every year, as it is paradise for anyone who goes there. Stand there under all the majesty proclaimed by our deity and you'll understand why this must, in honesty and truth, be called a monument to God.

At high noon the valley grows mellow and warm under the brilliant desert sun. At most the thermometer registers in the low 90's and even then there is immediate relief from the never-oppressive heat to be found in the nearest shade, where the line between coolness and heat is as definite and finely drawn as the shadow itself. When these shadows are at their minimum, the red buttes and mesas reach upward in all their stark beauty, unadorned except by their stern lines and rich coloring.

I have rested there on the porch at Harry Goulding's lodge and watched the sun go down. Slowly, as if being heated by some internal fire that has flamed to intensity over the long day, the monuments become a violent and bloodlike red. They seem about to burst with their inward fury and spew their coloring about the landscape.

Then abruptly it is over. The sun makes its last retreat, sinking behind Old Baldy. And, as it disappears, a color change takes place as suddenly as if you had snapped your fingers and all the players had been awaiting your cue. In a brief moment the flaming crimson has fled, and a deep-hued purple takes over. It grows in depth and intensity until darkness, when the monuments assume a role of great black silhouettes against the horizon.

In the mystery of the night, the buttes and mesas seem to appear as the ruins of great Grecian temples dating from the very beginning of time. And the shadows of their people dance among them.

At night, when the land breathes and sighs softly, whispering to you of its past, it is easy to realize the vastness of the chasm that lies between Monument Valley and our civilization. There is no thought or worry of distant wars, no regard of conflict. All is gentle and soft and close. The valley has lain silent while all the fires of civilization have swept by and burned themselves out. Countless days and nights have settled there and caressed its features. To be there, to feel the pulse of the valley, is to realize the gold of your days. It is as though you were lifted away from the tedious

"Mike" Goulding, 1934
PHOTOGRAPH BY DUDY

Harry Goulding, 1939

and common things of our age. When you have walked in the brilliant sunshine of the valley of the monuments, thought for a moment of its flaming magic at sundown, or stood silent in the silver splendor of its haunted moonlight, it seems as though you have touched upon, and flirted with, the eternal.

There is joy and gladness there. There is hope and the bringing of a great inward calm. Monument Valley is Peace. Monument Valley is Eternal. Monument Valley is our God—the Land of Room Enough and Time Enough.

Sand dunes in Monument Valley

PHOTOGRAPH BY GIBBS M. SMITH

A NOTE TO THE FOURTH EDITION

REVERIE...

The view from Today has one distinct advantage over the view from Yesterday. The years in between. Years full of experiences. So now in my reverie the facts are cluttered with ghosts...

In 1955 THE SEARCHERS came to Monument Valley. Hollywood, under the direction of John Ford, arrived to film Alan LeMay's wonderful book. Texas never looked so good!

By then I had married the girl of the dedication and had commenced a career of trying to mold sixth graders. From our home near Denver Lois and I were able to visit the Valley more often and thus were there for awhile during the filming.

The entire crew had set up tent camp just below Goulding's and through the humor of a clever sign maker we were able to stand at the corner of Hollywood and Vine. Harry usually went out to the day's location in one of the Jeep station wagons he used in the early days for visitor trips into the Valley. He always invited us to come along so we got an intimate taste of Hollywood magic at work.

Harry made sure the Navajos got involved as much as possible. That was always his first concern. For hours he watched and admired the actors at work. He liked to say, "That Wayne feller sure can act!"...

Harry had a dog that seemed to share ownership of the Lodge. A small black poodle, which was especially incongruous for a Goulding dog. He named it "Hi-yu-ee". The evening meal was in the dining room, where Victor McLaglen had his YELLOW RIBBON fist fight.

We still ate on wooden picnic tables with a million mementoes crowding the walls. After dinner, hanging around and sharing stories, Harry would usually ask if we'd like to see his dog play the old upright piano. He'd turn back the cover to the keys, pull out the piano bench and say, "Play the piano, Hi-yu-ee". The poodle would race across the room, jump on the bench, and run the length of the keyboard, then back to the floor. I can still see Harry beaming – and encouraging an encore...

Monument Valley is always red. Everybody agrees to that. Designed from red sanstone. But ponder this. Monument Valley is also blue. Broad skies are never as blue as when they're a backdrop to Train Rock and Mitchell Butte and the rest. And Monument Valley is white. Anything from scattered skiffs to great swelling balls of white clouds framing the views. Sometimes they blot out the sun and create great pools of reddened black on the valley floor, a negative cloudscape.

In some ways best of all, Monument Valley is green. Come August with the monsoon rains from the Gulf of California, life is given to the Valley in unexpected plenty. Miraculous plants in wondrous variety make a green carpet of infinite shades of green extending to far horizons...

In 1971 we discovered the turn-off road had been paved all the way up the imposing incline to the Trading Post. We drove up so easily and parked below the post sign. Too easily. End of an initiation ritual.

The old approach road was all curves and undulations, contour-loving. Climaxed by the final imposing task of climbing to the shelf without stalling-out. Stop, pause, shift to lowest gear. Convince yourself, deep breath, and go full throttle for the wild dash to arrive on the uneven sandstone area in front of the dining room. Elation. Made it again. Getting there was all the fun!...

Harry spoke often of the Land of the Sleeping Rainbow. To him Monument Valley was first the one with the Mittens. Secondly, the whole bigger land corralled by the Fence. Finally, the horizon-bound land in every direction, extending just as far as adventure beckoned. The Moss Backs and Bear's Ears to the North. Train Rock and Jacobs Thumb westward, and Copper Canyon if you were lucky enough to be able to go that far. Also, Organ Rock and Tsegi-a-Tsosi, the Long Slim Woman Canyon.

We went that way, chasing Harry's rainbows. Wandered all the way to then-remote Paiute Farms along the San Juan. Camped nearby in utter silence. Saw the night put the rainbow to sleep...

If you would really see a view of Monument Valley, Harry told us, get to Muley Point. Beyond the Valley of the Gods, up the escarpment. You can see everything from there, including yesterday and get to Muley Point. Beyond the Valley of the Gods, up the escarpment. You can see everything there, including yesterday and tomorrow.

So we camped one night at Muley. Got there in time to be immersed in sunset as we looked over the Goosenecks. He was right – all of Monument Valley was stretched out on an invisible canvas. We bathed that evening in a pothole, had a canned banquet, and reminisced with the spirits, then spent the night canopied with stars too numerous to count. When dawn came we looked south to catch the sun's return once again to the monuments. We were present at the dawning of Creation. It was a fresh, new world made rich by such things as Muley Point and Monument Valley...

We escorted 52 French visitors who had come from Strasbourg. Of course they wanted to see the legend. So we planned a night at the Lodge. I had arranged for a 16 mm copy of SHE WORE A YELLOW RIBBON to be delivered there. That evening we sat in the dining room and watched the film that took place, in part, right in that room. I don't suppose they understood why it meant so much to me. We invited Navajo neighbors as our guests. Every time they saw the cavalry and John Wayne they cheered for the Indians. That's fair...

A group of senior citizens from St. Paul's Methodist Church in my hometown back in Iowa asked that I guide them to the Valley of Monuments. We stayed in the original lodge units up on the shelf, west of the Trading Post. Before turning in I suggested if anyone would be willing to get up at 5:30 and join me they would see a spectacular event. Sunrise. Expected a few. All 47 were there.

Now they share a memory with me. Harry would have been proud of that sunrise. It was marvelous. I kept it. It's on the wall of my home. In memoriam. To Harry...

The two of us drove into the Valley, thinking hard on all the times before when the road had been more a promise than a fact. Where we couldn't come except via 4-wheel drive. When Harry always charged everyone a little extra and converted it into groceries which he shared with any Navajo we met along the way. Plus water he carried in to save them the long trip to his well.

This time we got only as far as the parking overlook to the distant

Totem Pole and found the road blocked from going further. I wished I hadn't discovered why. The Marlboro people were filming a commercial and motorcycles were churning up the red dunes. I liked John Wayne better...

I think of all of these – and so many more. In my reverie a Monument Valley sunrise is just as profound as it ever was. A sunset still depicts the meaning of things eternal. Snow lies just as white and perfect between the Mittens. The Totem Pole still baffles, and defies the law of gravity, while the Yei-ba-chai perform their endless dance in silence. That view of the Castle just after crossing Monument Pass heading north still pulls me over to the side and demands a measured look. Agathlan shows no sign of aging and Owl Rock stares on sightlessly from the mesa top.

And the Tall Man With the Sheep still gazes from the shaded porch of his trading post, squints against the distance to the line of monuments he always called The Fence, sees a fast moving faraway trail of dust and says with more than a trace of irony, "Oh, that's just some darn fool who thinks he's seeing Monument Valley"...

On my very first trip into the Valley, while preparing for the resulting manuscript, Harry pointed east to a pair of distant features. "Dick, that's Liggett Mesa. A pretty place, at the far edge of Monument Valley. And that pinnacle just north of it is Rooster Rock. It's a long way over there. Hard to get to."

Ever since, I've wanted to get to Liggett Mesa and Rooster Rock. Never have. Next to impossible in the past, many restrictions now against leaving your car and walking. So I still haven't gotten there, to the edge of the world. To realize Harry Goulding's words filled with mystery and romance and promise. It's my personal will o' the wisp. It's part of the legend.

I will someday. I'll keep trying. I still have time enough and the Valley has room enough...

BIBLIOGRAPHY

BOOKS

American Guide Series, *Utah, a Guide to the State,* Writers' Program, WPA, Hastings House, New York, 1941.

American Guide Series, *Arizona, a Guide to the State,* Writers' Program, WPA, Hastings House, New York, 1940.

BERNHEIMER, CHARLES L., *Circling Navajo Mountain with a Pack Train,* Doubleday, Page, and Co., Garden City, N. Y., 1924.

GILLMOR, FRANCES, and LOUISA WADE WETHERILL, *Traders to the Navajo,* Houghton Mifflin Co., Boston and New York, 1934.

GREY, ZANE, *Tales of Lonely Trails,* Harper Brothers, New York and London, 1922.

LEE, WILLIS THOMAS, *Stories in Stone,* D. Van Nostrand Co., New York, 1926.

LIPPS, OSCAR H., *The Navajos,* Torch Press, Cedar Rapids, Iowa, 1909.

PEATTIE, RODERICK, editor, *The Inverted Mountains,* Vanguard, New York, 1948.

STEGNER, WALLACE, *Mormon Country,* Duell, Sloan, & Pearce, New York, N. Y., 1942.

MAGAZINES

CLARK, NEIL M., "Desert Trader," *Saturday Evening Post,* vol. 219, pp. 36-37 (March 29, 1947).

CLARK, NEIL M., "Valley of Mystery," *Saturday Evening Post,* vol. 222, pp. 40-41 (March 25, 1950).

BREED, JACK, "Flaming Cliffs of Monument Valley," *National Geographic Magazine,* vol. 88, pp. 452-461 (October, 1945).

BULLETINS

BAKER, ARTHUR A., "Geology of the Monument Valley-Navajo Mountain Region, San Juan County, Utah," Geological Survey Bulletin 865 (1936), U. S. Department of the Interior.

GREGORY, HERBERT E., "The Navajo Country," U. S. Geological Survey Water-Supply Paper 380 (1916), U. S. Department of the Interior.

HALL, ANSEL FRANKLIN, "General Report on the Rainbow Bridge-Monument Valley Expedition of 1933," University of California Press, Berkeley, Calif.

INDEX

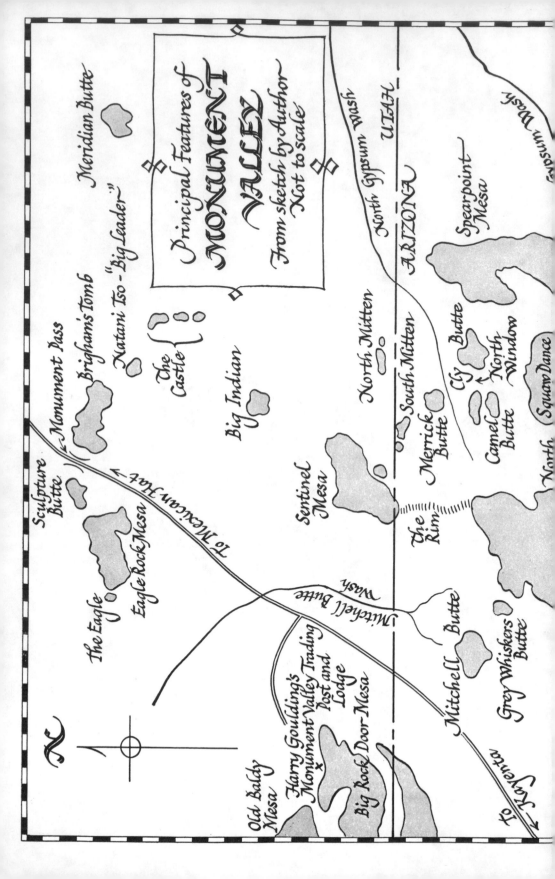

Principal Features of
MONUMENT VALLEY
From sketch by Author
Not to scale

N

To Mexican Hat →

UTAH
ARIZONA

North Gypsum Wash

Gypsum Wash

Meridian Butte

Brigham's Tomb

Natani Tso - "Big Leader"

Monument Pass

Sculpture Butte

The Castle

Big Indian

Eagle Rock Mesa

The Eagle

Sentinel Mesa

North Mitten

South Mitten

The Rim

Merrick Butte

Cly Butte

North Window

Camel Butte

Spearpoint Mesa

Squaw Dance

North

Mitchell Butte Wash

Mitchell Butte

Grey Whiskers Butte

Old Baldy Mesa

Harry Goulding's Monument Valley Trading Post and Lodge

Big Door Mesa

Big Rock Door Mesa

To Kayenta →